WHY THERE MUST BE A REVOLUTION IN QUEBEC

People's Publishing

NC Press publishes books and pamphlets that will be of assistance in the Canadian People's struggle for national liberation.

In the production of our books, we try to put into practice the attitudes and techniques of people's struggle. While the author must receive the main credit (and take the main responsibility) for a book, the production is a social experience involving the contributions of many others.

When we accept a manuscript, an editorial board is chosen to review it - a board of working people who donate their time to see to it that our books are accurate and understandable to the people. When the manuscript is ready, it goes into production and finally into print. But there is much more work to do: promotion, selling, shipping and invoicing.

To all those who helped on this book, our special thanks.

Your comments and criticisms are invited:

In order to produce better books, we need the assistance of our readers. If you have any comments or criticisms, of this or any other NC Press books please let us know about them.

WHY THERE MUST BE A REVOLUTION IN QUEBEC

by Léandre Bergeron
translated by Sheldon Lipsey
edited by Caroline Perly

NC PRESS LIMITED
TORONTO 1974

First published as
Pourquoi Une Révolution au Québec,
Éditions Québécois, 1972.

Also by the same author. . .
The History of Quebec — A Patriote's Handbook
The History of Quebec — In Pictures!
Petit Manuel d'Histoire du Québec
Histoire du Québec, Illustrée, No. 1 & 2
L'Histoire du Québec en 3 Régimes

The Author: Léandre Bergeron teaches Québécois Literature at Sir George Williams University in Montreal. In 1970 he wrote, published and distributed his now famous *Petit Manuel d'Histoire du Québec,* published in English as *The History of Quebec — A Patriote's Handbook* by NC Press. Léandre Bergeron is co-founder of Éditions Québécoises, Éditions de l'Aurore, and Diffusion-Québec which publish and distribute much of the best social and political writing and music coming out of Quebec today.

ISBN 0-919600-16-6

New Canada Publications, a division of NC Press Limited, Box 4010, Station A, Toronto, Ontario.

Printed in Canada by Union Labour

CONTENTS

INTRODUCTION

After the publication of *The History of Québec, a Patriote's Handbook*, I felt a logical follow-up would be the study of the structure of Québécois society. The *Handbook* having given the broad outline of the historical development, the next book should analyze the specific structures of that society, political, economic, social and cultural and the very specific contradictions that lead to the next historical stage, the overthrow of capitalism and the establishment of an independent socialist Quebec.

I also felt in 1972 when this book was written that there was an absolute need to explain revolution and the revolutionary process. These terms had been given a very derogatory meaning with the October crisis of 1970 and the subsequent massive attack of the federal and provincial governments against radical social change. What is revolution *really* ? Why is there such a thing as revolution? Who is revolutionary? Who is not? Why should the workers make a revolution? Who is reactionary? Where is everyone of us situated in the revolutionary process? These are some of the questions that I felt had to be discussed in simple straightforward language.

I choose the dialogue form because it is live, dynamic and straightforward. Also, this present dialogue is to a great extent the transcript of discussions I've had with many Québécois workers and students over a period of five years.

I did not visualize an English translation, feeling that the discussion throughout the book was very specifically Quebec-based, and therefore could not be for others, the handbook that it was to be for many Québécois. But the editors of NC Press convinced me that by adding certain explanatory notes and modifying certain passages, Canadian workers in general would not only be able to see how things are developing in Quebec, but also apply to their specific situation the relevant content; since of course the fundamental contradiction is the same for both Québécois and Canadian workers.

I would like to stress in this introduction a point I try to make at the end of the book. The national struggle going on in Quebec is not a struggle against Canadians but against a specific political structure that is alienating both Canadians and Québécois. We must all keep in mind that the fundamental struggle is the same for both, the struggle against capitalists, local and especially foreign, U.S.-based since the latter are the big wheels of the system.

My hope is that this translation of *Pourquoi Une Révolution au Québec* will help Canadian workers and students understand Québécois workers so that the common interests of both will be a uniting force against our common enemy, American imperialism.

Léandre Bergeron,
September 1974

Translator's note on the language:
The language of this book, with all its double negatives, faulty syntax and "vulgar" or "obscene" language, is as faithful a rendition as possible of the "bad French" of the original version. As the author suggests in a short postface to that edition, we must bring the discussion out of the academic ivory tower and into the street. "We must begin sometime, somewhere, to write the way people write, and stop writing the way the dominant class demands in order to perpetuate its rule."

PART ONE

The Structure
of Oppression

Growing Up

What? A revolution? Blood in the streets, people getting killed? No thanks. Revolutions are all the same. Look at Cuba, Algeria. What's going on in Ireland right now? Revolutions mean violence, and I don't want violence.

Don't worry. It won't come if we don't want it. A revolution isn't something that comes from outside. It comes because the majority of exploited people have had enough and start taking action. If you don't want things to change — tied to your job and all that — well, it won't happen. If you and thousands of others aren't convinced that things have to change and that you have to do whatever it takes to do it, well, things won't change, and there won't be a revolution.

A revolution isn't first and foremost streets flowing with blood, even if that's the picture TV gives us. The violence of the Second World War, with its 45 million casualties, wasn't for revolution. The two shouldn't be confused, even if frequently there are violent actions in certain phases of the revolution.

So what is it?

When you were twenty and you said to your father, "Hey dad, leave me alone. I'm big enough to make my own decisions," you made a revolution. Your personal revolution. He had crushed you in his role as a father as it's defined in our society. You overthrew his authority and you took on responsibilities. You declared your freedom from him. Oh, maybe you consulted him after that, but you wouldn't obey him. You changed the framework of your relationship. *That's* a revolution.

A revolution is a change in the structure of relationships. With your father, the relationship was one of authority-obedient child, or dominator-dominated. By breaking it, with all the fighting and bawling-out that it took, you established a new, one-to-one relationship. Before, it was:

father

son

Now it is:

older man   younger man

You may have had to shake your fist at him. Or else he understood in the first place.

That was your revolution. If you haven't made it yet, that's serious. There are some people who instead of making this personal revolution against paternal authority throw themselves into political activity, to find a safety-valve for their "misunderstood son" frustrations. Their so-called political activity smacks of it. They don't act like responsible men and women who understand the need for social change, but rather like teenagers mad at daddy.

Okay, okay! What about the revolution?

Revolution is a change in the structures of society.

That sounds good but it doesn't mean anything.

Do we agree on the word "society?"

It's, say, all Québécois, the six million living in the territory we call Quebec.

We could say "Quebec social grouping," as they put it in academic terms at the University of Quebec.

Okay "Quebec society." That means that the individuals who are part of this community have relationships among themselves.

Yes, but if you look at it properly, you see that Quebec society is not isolated. We have our culture, language, customs, ways of doing things. But economically — *hold on, we are not isolated at all.* In fact, we are so *un*isolated that our economic activity is entirely decided and controlled by other communities. And from a political point of view, . . . confederation . . . well, that's another community organizing us.

A culture without a political and economic base quickly turns into folklore.

What counts in the final analysis is economics. If half the world has to "talk American" and drink Coke it's because American society has extended its economic domination over a lot of countries.

When you control the economic base of a country, you can take political control very fast. After that, the culture can be plucked — like a ripe fruit.

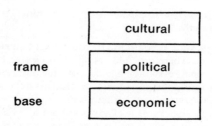

In Quebec, we Québécois have never had control of our economy *or* our politics. One hardly knows anymore what's left of our culture, except that we're a people, that we speak a special sort of French, that we always lost. We define ourselves much more by what we don't have than by what we have. But we want to change that now.

Quebec society is a nation.

A nation is a society on a given territory, with its own language, traditions, its own way of seeing the world, of thinking, of acting.

But from an economic point of view. . .

From an economic point of view the Quebec nation is a colony in the American empire.

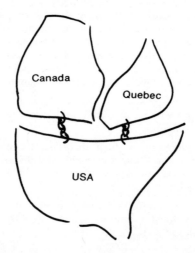

The American Empire!

The largest empire the world has ever seen. Asia, Africa, Latin America. But its most important colony is Canada — and that colony-within-a-colony, Quebec. More than one quarter of U.S. investment overseas is in Canada and Quebec. What does that mean for us?

Quebec serves the interests of the American community first. Our resources are handed to them at an incredible rate. And in return, they teach us to be good consumers of *their* products manufactured with *our* resources for *their* profits.

From a political point of view . . .

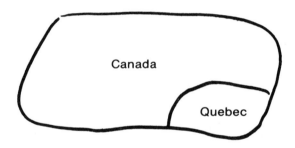

Quebec is part of a greater whole. But, a nation should be an independent entity, engaged in relations with other nations, as equals. Right now Quebec is a part of the American empire as we just said. But it's also a part of the country or state of Canada which is comprised of two nations, Quebec and an English-speaking nation which doesn't even have a name. I guess it's just called Canada. However, the two nations of Canada are not on an equal basis. Confederation, which is a political structure set up by the British to unify their colonies in North America and protect them from a direct U.S. takeover, puts Canadians in a position of dominating the Québécois. *We're* tired of it. They're starting to get tired of it, too.

A nation should control its economy, its politics, and its culture?

Yes.

Bourgeois Democracy

I just don't believe it! We live in a democracy. Democracy is government by the people. The people elected their members of Parliament didn't they? Everybody's happy except a few cry babies. We don't need revolution.

Whoa! Let's make a distinction. There are democracies and democracies. For the Greeks, who invented the word, there was a democracy for free men, who were hardly a tenth of the population. The others, the slaves, submitted to the dictatorship of those who enjoyed democracy. Today it's much the same. We have democracy, but democracy for who? Democracy for the bosses. *They* feel they're in a democracy, and it *is* a democracy for them. But for those who work for them, it's a dictatorship. Bourgeois democracy is democracy for the bourgeoisie and dictatorship for the people.

Well, *I* get a vote. I ain't a slave.

How many years have St-Henri and the other slum neighbourhoods been voting?

Ever since there's been voting in Quebec.

That's a long time. At least since these neighbourhoods have been around — more than a hundred years. So you think the people in these neighbourhoods have been voting themselves into poverty for a hundred years, while the bourgeois in Westmount and Outremont vote themselves into wealth? Seems to me that if voting worked the way you'd like to think it does, the working-class neighbourhoods would vote, if not for absolute happiness, at least for being better off.

That's not how it works.

That's right. The vote that we know is wool over our eyes, to have us think that democracy is for us too. But it's a democracy of the bourgeois and it's for them alone.

You're repeating yourself.

Relations of Production

Just now we said that a revolution is a change in the structures of society. We agreed on the word "society." Let's go on to the word "structure."

First, the structures of a society are not obvious. If they were, it would be simple. Imagine you're looking at a house. You see the general shape, the colour, the windows. Maybe there are awnings that make it very nice, and balconies. But awnings and balconies don't say anything about the structure of the house, and I'd even say they keep us from seeing it.

It's the same for a society. At first glance, one would even say there is no structure. That there are people, period. Men, women, children all over the place, who move around any way they like.

People scattered like a pack of cards thrown on the ground. Now I ask you, where are you in the structure? You answer, "I dunno. There isn't even a structure."

Don't answer for me.

So answer.

Never mind, go on.

You don't see an obvious structure. Me neither. All the same, we don't do whatever we want. There are things we do out of necessity that come from *relationships. Social relationships.* The kid crying on the doorstep because his mommy said he couldn't go out, the dog following his master like a sheep, the guy washing dishes at the Select restaurant, the janitor taking out the garbage cans, the boss chewing out his employees. If people really acted the way they wanted to, they wouldn't do any of these things. But they do what they do because there are certain *social relation-*

ships that make them do it. The crying kid submits to the relationship of domination by his mother, the dog by his master, the dishwasher by the boss. . .

And if you look closely at the relationships between people and also between groups of people, you realize that the main relationship in our society is a relationship of domination. It's what we could call a *vertical relationship*.

Find me other relationships, find me a horizontal relationship, a relationship of equals.

In what area?

In the area of work.

Well, the guys in the shop, we're all equal.

You're there to do different jobs side by side, okay. You

feel equal to the other guys. But you're just carrying out a given job, without your having decided on the organization of the work.

But in the overall work process, you're in a vertical relationship with the boss.

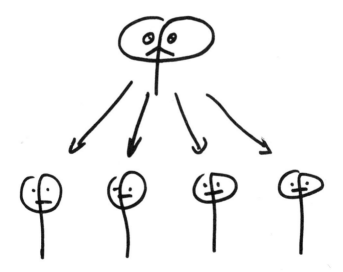

Who organises your shop?

The boss.

Who checks your time card?

The boss.

Who pays you?

The boss.

Who sells the things you make?

The boss.

In other words, your job is to do things for the boss. Material is to be turned into products, with the help of tools. You guys, you're the "human energy" ingredient.

Human energy? Animal energy! If work were humane...

Why isn't it humane?

Because they treat us like machines.

What would you change to be treated like human beings?

Not just doing boring work. Not being bossed around all the time. Having a say in things.

Taking part in the organizing of your work.

If that's what you mean, okay.

You want to change the structures of the work process. You want to decide as much as the boss. You don't want the relationship of domination any more. You don't want the vertical relationship any more. You want to make a revolution. You're a revolutionary!

Hold on. I said I wanted to take part with the boss.

Does your boss work?

Yes, he organizes my work.

That's not work.

Come on.

Organizing the work of others is not work. It's using carefully guarded knowledge to dominate other people so you won't have to work yourself. A boss is a boss. Someone who tells you what to do and pays you a pittance isn't a worker. He's an exploiter.

Jeezus!

Whatever is "humane" in the work process, the decisions to be made about the means of production, the boss takes away from you, monopolizes, keeps for himself. To keep you in this subhuman state, a machine for carrying out tasks.

You mean we workers could do the organizing ourselves, and then we'd be treated like human beings?

There wouldn't *be* any more boss.

No more boss?

If you guys did together the organizational work he keeps for himself, he'd have to leave — or become a worker same as the rest.

Hey, can you see a boss working?

Do him good!

Kee-rist!

You wouldn't have any more vertical relationships. They'd all be horizontal.

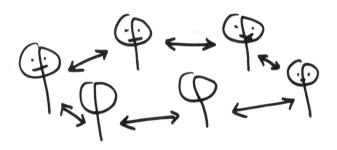

There'd be no more bosses.

We'd all be bosses.

If you're all bosses, there's no more boss. You'd all be workers, working and organizing your work. That's what a revolution is all about.

Impossible. Workers aren't smart enough.

You say you're not smart enough.

Well, me maybe. The other guys . . .

Why just you?

Yeah . . . But the bosses wouldn't want it.

Why should they?

What they got, they don't want to let go of.

Why should they?

So, what then?

So, you ask them if they'll please hand over the power of organization of work to those entitled to it.

So, they say no. Then we pound the shit out of them.

Why shouldn't you?

But they don't give in so easy. They call their lawyers and the police. Then it's the judges with injunctions. The government gets in on it. It'd be like a strike.

Why should the government get involved?

Because we need an arbitrator.

An arbitrator?

Between both sides. . .

Bullshit! You just said *the bosses* call the government. Wouldn't it be the government protecting your boss' "private property"?

Democracy. . .

Democracy again?!

Okay, okay. What is it then?

Social Relations at Home

Let's get back to our structures. In the society we know, the structures of domination we've seen in your work are everywhere. And it's no accident. If they were found only at work, they wouldn't last very long. They have to be everywhere, so that the mentality is maintained.

The domination of man over woman, parents over children, is important for "good upbringing," "preparation for life" — serving the boss.

When women begin to free themselves from men's

yoke, when children begin to shake off the family, our toleration of domination and exploitation in other relationships will break down. And the revolution will be that much nearer. It's coming fast anyway.

At home:

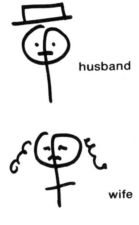

husband

wife

The couple

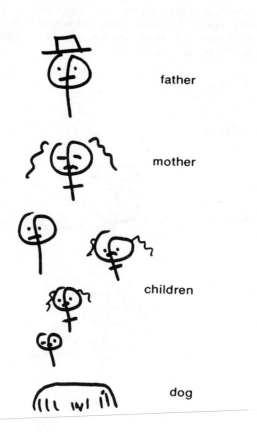

father

mother

children

dog

The family

My kids won't listen to me anymore.

Good.

My wife won't want to be bossed around anymore.

Good.

Yeah, but listen! I get kicked in the ass at work. Who am I gonna take it out on?

On your boss. The guy who kicked you.

Yeah, but the little woman'll take advantage. To make love now, she'll have to feel like it, too. What kind of life is that?

The beginning of *real* life.

I'll have to do the dishes . . .

Good. When you don't have a slave at home anymore, you'll refuse to be one at the shop.

Revolution's tough going.

The revolution will be complete, or it won't happen at all.

Goddam professor's talk!

Look at Russia. They started out well in 1917. The factory councils they called *soviets* took over the factories and began to manage them. But the revolution immediately came under attack. As the attacks continued the Bolshevik party didn't carry the revolution through and reverted to the same authoritarian means as their predecessors. And today, in spite of the economic progress made, Russia finds itself with a new class struggle. They need another revolution.

Never mind your speeches on Russia. This is Quebec, and I don't like to think I got no authority over my wife and kids.

You haven't got any authority over them.

But I'm the father.

Hell with the father. Make democracy work in your family first. All you can claim for yourself is a greater responsibility for your actions, because you have more experience.

It'll never work.

It'll work for the time being — until the family itself disappears as an old, outmoded institution. Like marriage.

You're nuts.

Social Relations in the Streets

Let's go out of the house.

In the street:

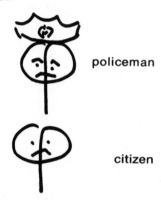

policeman

citizen

Well, that's clear!

The policeman represents the Authority that maintains the existing social order. He is not *the* Authority, he's only the enforcer.

That's why he's called an officer.

An officer of the "peace". The peace that's imposed on us.

You've already noticed how the police are different from one neighbourhood to the next. In working-class neighbourhoods, the cops are tough guys. Real bosses. But in Westmount, they're real nice to the people that live there. It's "good morning" and "nice day" all over the place. Servants of the people in rich neighbourhoods and dogs to everybody else.

They "serve and protect" the property of those who have against those who haven't.

Social Relations in the Market Place

The police protect the stores.

Policeman guards pile of rocks near Ayers Plant, as strikers defend themselves against police and strike-breakers, Lachute Strike - Ayers Plant, May 1947.

Well, that's worthwhile.

No.

Whaddya mean, no?!

Stores should be completely open, so that everyone can go in and take what he needs.

Are you nuts?!

Stores are full of consumer goods. Since workers made them, workers should own them. So it would be perfectly reasonable for you to take them from the stores, free of charge.

That's stealing.

Can you steal from yourself? You guys assemble motors in your shop. You and all the others who have had a part in the manufacture of these motors are the owners. It's only right. They certainly don't belong to the boss — he's never even seen them. So, you need a motor. You go into a store, and there's the motor you assembled. What do you do? You take it. Because you put it together, because it's your share in society.

I pay for it with the wages I made putting it together.

Don't you sound a bit silly?

No.

How much do the parts cost when they get to your workbench?

About $50.

Once you've assembled the motor, how much is it worth?

$100.

And your wages for assembling it?

About two hours. $7 or so.

You've added $50 to the value of the motor with your work. How much is it worth in the store?

$180.

You've tripled the value of the parts by turning them into a motor, and you're going to pay *twenty-six and a half times* the pittance you got for making it.

Ouch!

Ouch is right!

But why would it belong to me more than to the guy who sells it or the guys who made the parts?

That's true. It belongs to *all* those who worked on it or transported it. That makes it a social product. It even belongs a bit to your wife who took care of you so that you could produce it. In fact it belongs to all women workers, all men workers, and their husbands and wives.

That's just about everybody!

Everybody but the bourgeois — the bosses, the presidents of large companies, the big shots who organise other people's work!

And they're the people who call themselves the owners of the things everybody else produces. It's all upside-down.

Turning things right side up, that's revolution.

Revolution is workers organizing their work, appropriating the raw materials and the tools, and distributing their products according to the people's needs. . .

Yes. But we're getting ahead of ourselves. Back to our structures of oppression. We said that on the street the cop represents Authority over the people.

What about in the alleys?

It's a man who would like to grab a woman.

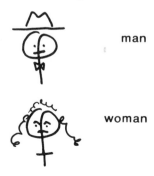

man

woman

Or a gang grabbing a little girl to get her pants down.

Or the guy big enough to attack a little guy who might have money in his pockets.

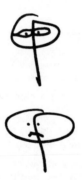

Maybe the guy's unemployed and he's hungry.

In most cases, he's got nothing and he's just taking what society won't give him.

It's a way of taking what belongs to him. So it's not stealing. Is that it?

It depends on who you steal from. If an unemployed man takes a worker's wages by hitting him in an alley, that's stealing. But if he takes a bourgeois' belongings that's not stealing. It's taking back what is his.

It's a bit like workers who take over their factory and throw the boss out.

Yes and no. The individual action of the unemployed man doesn't change the structure. He grabs a few crumbs, standing a good chance of ending up behind bars.

But the takeover of a factory by workers eliminates the boss from the work process itself.

So maybe you mean the rise in the crime rate is 'cause there are "bad guys" who want to take from the "good guys." You mean there are more and more dispossessed who just want to take back their share from society.

In general, yes. For most kinds of theft, that's why. Now, if you're talking about rape or murder, that's another story.

You mean the guys who knock over a bank or a grocery store . . .

Take a look in our prisons. Most of the guys are in there for that kind of crime. And most of them are from the working class.

You can say that again. I did six months once. I can tell you, most of the guys in there were guys like me. But there was a gang of them that were unemployed for a long time.

The unemployed are part of the working class. They're just workers who don't have jobs. Workers who are part of the "reserve labour force" needed by the capitalist system.

Social Relations at School

Now let's go into the school.

In class   In the schoolyard

principal

secretaries

In the principal's office

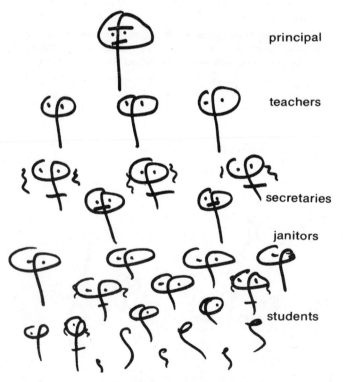

principal

teachers

secretaries

janitors

students

School group portrait

If I remember rightly, that's how it was. Dictatorship.
The principal. Christ, he scared us! And the lady teachers
that were so nice to him! Shaking in their pants. So they took
it out on us. And out in the schoolyard, we'd beat up the girls
or the little kids. Or else we'd smash the swings or the windows. I can see now why we felt like smashing everything.
But all the same I did learn to read and write.

But especially we learned our place. In a vertical structure. What really counted, eh? What did it mean, being a
good student? Remembering everything they taught us?
No. Knowing how to listen, how to follow orders. To be
good. To do what the Man wanted so that later we'd know
how to follow orders at the shop, at the office, in the government.

The bosses' sons went to school too.

Yes, but in what kind of schools? *Private* schools,
where they learn not to follow orders, but to *give* them. Go
take a look around Selwyn House[1]. No long hair there.
White shirts, striped ties, blazers. All in uniform. Discipline. No one slouching around in the halls. "Yes sir,"
"excuse me sir." Why? Because becoming bourgeois, becoming a boss, doesn't just happen. These sons of the
bourgeois are the future generals of the work army and generals are not born. They're made. He learns to stand up
straight and have a good command of the language . . .

**Goddam, it's important the way you talk, when you think
of it. Knowing how to use nice-sounding words, *that's* authority. People listen to you. It impresses people. It's like the
Frenchmen who came here. Us guys stood there with our
mouths open, couldn't say a word.**

**Remember Trudeau in '72? He said "When you guys
learn to speak French properly, then we'll listen to you." But
it's not like that any more. Frenchmen don't impress us any
more. And Trudeau can go to hell. We're beginning to speak
up, here in Quebec.**

They taught us to keep quiet and follow orders. Then
they wanted to teach us nice, prissy French, like the Holy-
Name-of-Jesus-and-Mary nuns speak, telling us the language we spoke was like shit.

1 A private school in Westmount.

That's what makes the flowers grow!

How about thistles, with their little mauve flowers.

You know about horseshit, don't you?

I shovelled enough of it, when I was younger. But let's get back to our school. The boss' son learns to speak the master's language, to walk like a boss, stand like a boss, see the world as if it belongs to him, as if he had rights over the land and the people on it.

Now I see why we wanted to smash everything, and why we couldn't figure out why the rich kids didn't. Learning that everything belonged to them, where's us kids were learning that nothing would ever belong to us, except heaven when we died. Obedience, submission, respect for authority, charity. Jesus Lord Christ!

Schools are just training grounds. Some are for generals, others are for privates. Know your place. That's our school system.

But there are guys who manage to change sides.

True. The bourgeois are always ready to pick out the most intelligent workers and make them lieutenants. Their intelligence is useful — and they can say "anybody can be president of General Motors". Hey, in Williamstown, Massachusetts, there's a college for the kids of the richest people in the States. Nearly two hundred buildings for 1500 to 2000 students. You can see they're living pretty well. Theatres, gymnasiums, private apartments . . .

Well, let me tell you, half the students are sons of the super-rich, but the other half are super-intelligent sons from families of modest means. Why? So that the not-always-so-bright rich kids can pit their brains against them. Just in case intelligence does rub off . . .

And at the same time the poor kids are carving out careers for themselves. Tuition fees are about $5000 a year, but tuition for bright poor students is paid by bursaries that fall from heaven, just like that!

The Americans didn't discover anything new there. We had the same thing in the classical colleges. Sons of poor families had their schooling paid for by the village priest.

It's the same thing, except that the Americans are training the captains of industry, while our institutions of "learning" turn out missionaries and rois-nègres.[1]

It's all very well for you to say there's a vertical structure, as you call it, in schools. But you can't just throw it away. It'd be a mess!

That's true. Especially if you take it away at school without taking it away at home.

Even if it is done gradually, I don't see how you could do it. Kids'll be kids.

Within the existing system, yes. They're so inhibited that when they do get the chance, bang! They explode all over the place. Bringing up a child in our system is like trying to keep the steam in a boiling pot. As long as you hold the lid on, it's okay. You burn your fingers a bit, but that's all right. But if you lift the lid all at once, you get the steam right in your face.

Look at the violence we do to our children. "Don't touch your weewee. Eat your soup. Be quiet. Go to sleep. Get up. Down on your knees. Don't do this, don't say that. Kiss me. Say excuse me to your father. Kiss your sister. Come here so I can spank you. Make poopoo.

Hold yourself in. Not in front of our guests. Go to your room. Don't touch. I'll cut it off if you touch it again. Cover that up, it's not nice. Get dressed quickly. Sit quietly." A child's life is full of don'ts that bugger him up for life. We have complexes, neuroses, endless physical and mental illnesses.

The structures of oppression are an integral part of ourselves. We're loyal subjects of the system. We've been done over, remoulded, we obey. We cry over the love we can't find. We think we've found love when we find someone who's twisted the same way we are. We cry out for

1 The conquest of Africa by White colonialism advanced in two stages; first, a brutal military conquest and destruction of any nest of resistance, followed by an appeal for collaboration. While ostensibly maintaining their traditional position as leaders, certain tribal chiefs became, in fact, mere puppets of the colonialists. Such indigenous collaboration effectively camouflaged the extent of colonial domination.

happiness. We sing about it, cry about it. But it always seems so shortlived when it does come.

Hold on! I don't know where you're at now.

When we've been well brought up, we've been screwed up. We don't know how to relax, breathe, eat, make love, love others without possessing them, love nature without raping it, just being. We do what we don't want to do. It's as if we are outside ourselves. We lead the life we're *obliged* to live.

There have been sensitive souls, mutilated by their "good upbringing", who saw all this, in a flash. Listen to the poem *Accompagnement* by our poet Saint-Denys Garneau:

> *I walk beside a joy*
> *Beside a joy that is not mine*
> *A joy of mine which I cannot take*
>
> *I walk beside myself in joy*
> *I hear my footsteps in joy walking beside me*
> *But I cannot change places on the sidewalk*
> *I cannot put my feet in those steps and say:*
> > *"Look it is I."*
>
> *For the moment I am content with this company*
> *But secretly I plot an exchange*
> *By all sorts of devices, by alchemies*
> *By blood transfusions*
> *Displacement of atoms, by balancing tricks*
>
> *So that one day, transposed,*
> *I may be carried along by the dance of those steps of joy*
> *With the noise of my footsteps dying away beside me*
> *With the fall of my own lost step fading to my left*
> *Under the feet of a stranger turning down a side street.*

That's it. He feels it. He knows it. He tries gimmicks to change things, even poetry itself.

I thought poetry was . . .

Obviously, there are all kinds of poetry. From pure

marshmallow to navel-gazing. But there *are* poets who have something to say, who do have flashes of awareness.

You think you're gonna get me to read poetry now?!

No, no. I just wanted to give you some examples of guys who saw themselves, drew a picture of their interior, and showed it to people. Most of them didn't understand it. They didn't see that those guys they thought were crazy were describing, scientifically, the condition of "civilized" man . . .

Scientifically, **did you say?**

Just because you use imagery doesn't mean you're not being scientific. The physicist who draws a sketch of an atom is using images that really look very little like an atom. But we're digressing.

Just let me say we're beginning to understand the guys who're telling us our civilization is screwed up, that being civilized means being twisted. It hasn't always been that way, and it's not always going to be that way.

PART II

A History of Oppression

Primitive Democracy

Before man discovered agriculture and built up food reserves, he didn't function within structures of domination at all. It was primitive democracy. Take the Iroquois before the white man brought them "civilization": there were no decisions behind closed doors. The council made them, in front of everybody. The military chiefs were elected only for a certain war and lost their positions when the war was over. Women could vote.

The chiefs were not a land-owning class, separate from the people. Property was communal. The greatest quality a chief could possess was his devotion to the common good of the tribe.

Real leaders, right? Not dictators imposing an order based on class exploitation and if the chief began taking too many privileges, he was quickly dismissed. And to think that taking part in a war was always voluntary, that prisoners taken from the enemy were not reduced to slavery (i.e. providing free labour for their masters) but rather were invited to join the tribe.

They didn't bring up their children. They let them grow up. Children weren't made to name the things around them. They learned by imitating, at their own rate. Their bodies belonged to them. All that's to say that man has not always lived with structures of oppression.

Slavery, Feudalism, Wage Slavery

From the time agriculture was discovered, we've had civilization, and civilization has been the domination of one class over another . . .

Civilization has given rise to the exploitation of one group in society by another. First of all, the reduction of women to slavery, a gilded slavery in some cases, and then the enslavement of prisoners. Thanks to this slavery, man could pursue his inventions, improve his means of battling nature in order to survive and develop. Down through the centuries, the shape of exploitation changed. Slavery was replaced in the Middle Ages in Europe by the feudal system, and then towards the 18th century, with the invention of machines, by capitalism.

You mean to say the worker, even if he's driving a Mustang, is exploited just like the Roman slave?

Yes. On the face of it, the Roman slave belonged to his master but the modern industrial worker is free to sell his labour power as he wishes.

Under the slave system, there was at least some paternalism towards the slaves—the familiarity and condescension of rich people towards their servants. Slave owners at least in good times were obligated to look after their slaves from birth to death.

But capitalists give their workers a wage so as not to be bothered with them. The worker can feed his family or he can piss it away, the capitalists don't give a damn. There's always the reserve of workers, the unemployed, they can dip into. It's crude: "You wanna work for me? Okay, work. For so much money. If you don't produce—out, goodbye, we get somebody else."

That's how it is, all right!

All that is to say our civilization, ever since it has been civilization, had changed the forms of oppression but not its basic structure—a dominant minority of owners enjoying the fruits of the labour of the non-owning majority.

So then, you think now, after thousands of years, you're gonna change all that?!

Yes.

Public Archives of Canada

In the Revolutions of 1837-39 the people of Upper and Lower Canada rose up to fight back against the oppression of British imperialism. Here, a group of Patriotes are gathered at Beauharnois during their third offensive in November, 1838.

Are you an optimist!

The Canayen Under Three Regimes

It's happening right now, right around us. Here in Quebec, every day. The whole authoritarian system is crumbling at work, at home, in school. People won't have any more of it. They want to start making decisions in their lives and stop being workers following orders and consumers conditioned like rats in a laboratory. Have you talked to any teachers lately? The system isn't working any more. Kids don't want to listen. They don't want to be treated like jugs to be filled.

Look at what happened in May[1] right across Quebec. Workers took over cities, radio stations, hospitals.

Look at all the divorces these days, couples breaking up, kids leaving home, people freeing themselves from old ways of living and dressing . . .

Hey, wait a minute! You're mixing everything up.

It's all tied in. We're in the middle of a revolution!

Wha?

We agreed that since the discovery of agriculture we've been living within a structure of oppression. A minority dominating the majority to take the fruits of its labour from it, right?

Right.

We've gone from the slavery of ancient times to medieval serfdom, and now to the wage-earning of capitalism.

---

1 In the Spring of 1972, civil servants and teachers (210,000 in all), members of the Confederation of National Trade Unions (CNTU), Quebec Federation of Labour (QFL), and the Quebec Teachers' Corporation (CEQ) went on strike for better salaries and working conditions. The Bourassa government tried to break the strike through court injunctions. The strikers defied the injunctions and Bourassa replied by jailing the union leaders, Pepin, Laberge, and Charbonneau. Hundreds of thousands of Quebec workers retaliated by paralyzing the economy of Quebec, taking over towns, communication systems, and institutions.

Okay.

And now at this stage of capitalism, the exploited majority is upsetting the order of things.

No, no. Nothing's gonna change. You'll just get a new gang in power and you'll have the old exploitation in a new shape. Look at Russia.

Exactly. Because in Russia, as I said before, they didn't change the authoritarian structures. Now in China, they *are* . . .

Oh yeah, China . . . Mao decides everything . . .

Okay. Let's start closer to home. We'll get back to China in a minute. We Québécois are part of Western civilization, right?

Right.

We're caught in the same structures of oppression as the Americans, the French, the English, right?

Right.

But the advantage we have in Quebec is that as a people we have never really assimilated these structures or become part of them.

What do you mean?

Listen. Our ancestors came from France. The ones who came by choice were getting away from feudal oppression. Those who came through necessity, fugitives from justice and other "bad guys", were just as happy to leave. The French administrators and the clergy, as hard as they tried, couldn't entirely press the Canayens[1] into a feudal produc-

---

1 The word 'Canadien' is ambiguous. Under the French regime it referred to people of French origin born in Canada. After the Conqest it denoted the conquered people, the 70,000 French men and women who remained in Canada. A little later when England created Upper and Lower Canada the Canadien was robbed of his name, for 'Canadian' now included the English of Ontario. With Confederation and the creation of the Dominion of Canada, Canadians of French origin were obliged to call themselves French-Canadian to keep their identity. Today, 'Canadian' refers to the inhabitants of Canada from sea to sea. The French-Canadian who refuses to accept British, U.S. or Canadian colonialism any longer, who is conscious of a homeland of his own, must call himself Québécois.

tion system; the seigneurial system didn't quite work. The seigneurs could never exercise complete authority over the tenant farmers who were supposed to be tilling their land. The priests had a hard time collecting their tithe. Towards the 1740's the Canayens even staged a strike and didn't pay the tithe. Can you imagine?

The Canayen wouldn't take much bugging. When the French administrators tried to impose their laws, well, our man could just take to the woods. He could be gone for months, come back from the hunt with his bounty, sell it, take up working the land again. Independent? Man! Anti-authority, anti-government, anti-royalist. Not very Catholic. Leave him alone, or watch out. Not docile. Disobedient. Not a sheep.

Christ, that's the same as today!

I know. A Québécois makes a poor worker. He's hard-working, but at his own pace. He puts his heart in his work. But with a boss over him, he slows down his output, relaxes, every chance he gets. He breaks tools. He plays jokes. He's not serious. Ask English bosses, they'll tell you. Guys in Ontario — disciplined, serious workers, obedient . . .

What? That's a bit much!

Maybe so. But us Québécois, Blacks, Indians . . .

I don't get it. We're white, but we're down there with the blacks and the Indians . . .

Yes. In the French regime, it was quite clear. The French, the administrators, the clergy, agents of the fur companies never felt at home here, always felt they were agents of France, the metropolis. But the Canayens, the dispossessed who put down roots here, really felt at home along the river, working the land but especially taking to the woods.

There they came in close contact with the red man. When they didn't have to go to war and massacre these first inhabitants of the land, "to save New France for King Louis", they got along not too badly. The red man taught the Canayens not only the art of surviving in the forest but of living well, in tune with nature. They brought them medicine, recipes, and reinforced their taste for freedom.

I'll bet you that if there hadn't been a Plains of Abraham, our grandfathers here would have tossed the French administrators in the St. Lawrence during the French Revolution, made Quebec a sort of free territory. Not a free State, because they would have refused to have a State, just as the Indians wouldn't have a State.

You mean we're goddam savages.

Yes. We are in fact much closer to the red man than to the Westmount bourgeois.

Jesus Christ!

Especially as we've been colonized just like the Indians for two hundred years. Those guys on the reserves — we're brothers.

Hey, hey wait a minute! Explain that a bit more.

Because he was anti-feudalism and because he was near the forest, our Canayen was in fact an outlaw. So obviously, the Indian was an outlaw, too.

Now I understand why I did six months . . .

At the same time, the efforts of Canayen entrepreneurs to become bourgeois and really lock the Canayen people into the capitalist production system ended in catastrophe. The Canayen petit-bourgeois never had a chance, because the French administrators favoured the metropolis, the King of France, and the French bourgeoisie.

You mean we never had a bourgeoisie.

That's right. The intendent ordered workshops that made fur hats and coats burned down on orders from France. That took away all opportunities from the local entrepreneurs. They were driven back among the ordinary people. So, at the end of the French regime, there were 60,000 Canayens prevented by colonial law from reaching the next historical stage, the bourgeois stage, in which the local bourgeoisie takes over the economy of the colony, and then seizes political power from the mother country.

Meaning for us there was no bourgeois revolution like in other nations.

That's right. While the Americans were declaring their independence and by doing that overthrowing the authority of the king *and* the metropolis to make their bourgeois revolution, while the French bourgeoisie was getting ready to overthrow the monarchy, while the British bourgeoisie was undermining the power of the King, *we* were being conquered.

1760. Bango!

You bet. The Conquest cast us as an outlaw group in a structure of double oppression — national and class.

Holy Jesus!

The English became the bosses now. English administrators representing the English bourgeoisie maintaining the feudal order, to keep the Canayen under control.

. . . two regimes one on top of the other.

Foreigners preserving feudalism so that they could take over all trade (furs, then wood, for a start) and use the Canayens as cheap labour.

Seems to me I've read that somewhere already. In a little red-white-and-green book . . .

You see how it is? A bunch of Canayens stuck with English superiors. Very British? Bloody nonsense! They needed a good police force to keep our bunch of outlaws in line. There was the British army — and a clergy that wanted nothing better than to play policeman.

What? Priests are policemen?

Ideological police. The clergy has always had the role of brainwashing people to accept their place in the structure of exploitation.

At that period in history, the clergy was tied in with the monarchy and the whole feudal system. It wasn't hard for them to switch from the French monarchy to the English monarchy, especially as the French monarchy was shaking like hell at the time. All this was confirmed with the French Revolution in 1789. The clergy here went so far as to say . . .

. . . that thanks to the Conquest by the English the Canayen people had been saved from the terrible scourge of the Revolution.

Proving that the clergy of the period would rather

change nationality than go from a feudal to a bourgeois regime.

You can't get any more reactionary than that, can you? Not even wanting a bourgeois regime! And the bourgeois ain't revolutionaries either . . .

At the time, they were. They've gotten firmly into power since then. Now they're hanging on for dear life . . .

Now it's their turn to be reactionaries.

National Struggle In Quebec

The Clergy selling out to the English. Doesn't it remind you of some of our little bourgeois? Independence is the chance they've been dreaming about to become little bosses for the Americans in Quebec, to replace the English-Canadians.

Right on. A real bunch of 1760 priests . . .

If they think we haven't learned since then . . .

You see them in the Liberal party, eyeing the Parti Québécois. Then boing, they jump over. Just like frogs when the wind changes.

But they still call themselves Québécois.

A special kind of Québécois. The old clerics sold us out to the British in 1760, to the Americans after 1920. Today the "new clerics", looking very with-it in their mauve ties and pink shirts, are just a new generation jockeying for a better position in an "independent" Quebec. Above all else they'll defend their class interests. Petit-bourgeois who want to be big bourgeois.

Convince them that independence is impossible and they'll all go back to the Liberal party. They don't have the interests of the Quebec people at all at heart, or in their minds, or in their guts. In fact they don't give a damn about the Quebec people.

What these little-big men want is to move up in the structure. Take a ladder in an apple orchard. The bourgeois is on top. He picks the nicest apples for himself. He drops the not-so-nice ones down to the people at the bottom, who sweat to maintain the orchard. The petit-bourgeois is on the ladder, but just below the bourgeois. He gets to hold the basket, for which he receives a nice big apple now and then. It's not in his interest to change the apple-picking structure.

Okay, I get what you mean there by "class interests." The bourgeois, he's reactionary, he doesn't want nothing to change because he benefits most from this way of picking apples. The petit-bourgeois doesn't want to give up his place because . . . yeah.

Then the workers, well sure, they'd want the applepicking done with escalators going up and down, so's everybody in turn could take his little basket up and then go down the other side to eat his apples and keep up the orchard. Holy Mary! That's a revolution — replacing the old ladder with two escalators, one up, one down!

But for the petit-bourgeois, independence for Quebec would be painting the old ladder blue and sticking on fleur-de-lys decals they bought in Woolco, made in Japan.

Then the little basket gets to be a big Steinberg shopping basket.

And Steinberg still owns the basket.

The big Steinberg "S" up front, and the little "Q" behind.

Long live the Republic of Quebec!

And after all that we ain't one bit ahead.

We may even have gone backwards. Hey, imagine that bunch in power in a free Quebec. Can you just imagine what they'd do to consolidate their power? I think there'd be paddy wagons and jail cells, made by Dosco, "for the greater good of the Quebec nation". The question is whether we are going to leave the gaining of independence to the petit-bourgeoisie.

It'd be no picnic, I'll tell you.

The Nationalism of the Oppressors and The Nationalism of the Oppressed

Nationalism is the feeling of belonging to a society with its own characteristics — a common language, a territory, a way of looking at things, etc. In itself, this feeling is quite proper. As long as the differences between peoples are not antagonistic, that is, not based on exploitation there's no problem. So much the better if there are a lot of differences among peoples, hundreds of languages spoken by hundreds of nations of all colours. Life is that much enriched. Variety makes for fun. I wouldn't like to live in a world where everybody looked like a Yank.

Jee-zus!

But this feeling of belonging to a particular ethnic group is exploited in a class society by the dominant class, for its own interests. And it's always been that way.

Hitler was able to start the German bourgeoisie off building the Third Reich because this class, which had been humiliated and defeated by the French, English and American bourgeoisies, saw in the restoration of German honour and in imperial conquest a way of making big money. Think of the owners of the big steelworks in Germany. What a chance to make a comeback! Manufacturing cannons, army vehicles, planes, tanks. They were tickled pink.

Without the German bourgeoisie, there'd of been no Hitler!

The American bourgeoisie today is nationalistic, a na-

Metropolitan Toronto Central Library

Patriotes use guerrilla-style action to harass British soldiers marching on St. Charles, in the Revolution of 1837-39.

tionalism that justifies the domination of their nation over others. The word "patriot" (in the U.S. today) is associated with reactionaries and fascists. They want to concentrate all the capital they can in the United States and control the world. They'll call themselves 'internationalists' to look nice and not to frighten people, but in fact they're just like the old British and French colonialists. Today we call it imperialism.

But when it's not in their interests, the dominant class is anti-nationalist. Today in Quebec, the word "patriote" is associated with those "nasty revolutionaries". Why? Because this is the nationalism of an oppressed people struggling for liberation.

Wait a second. In Quebec there's a feeling of belonging that's been developing over the last fifteen years.

Well, it was always there, but it had always been exploited by the elite for its own advantage. Why don't we go back to the Conquest we were talking about before?

All right.

60,000 Canayens, a bunch of outlaws, now under British rule. The feeling of belonging to the Canayen people develops within the chains of colonial oppression. Being a Canayen *is* something. When the Americans were struggling for independence (1774-83), the Canayens supported them. When the French were revolting against the monarchy (1789-93), the Canayens supported them.

Then we had our own struggle against British oppression. A small elite — lawyers, doctors, notaries — emerged as a petit-bourgeoisie to lead the struggle against the British feudal structure. These were our Patriotes of the 19th century. In favour of bourgeois revolution but not a bourgeoisie, they had no economic power. They tried to be what they weren't. Bang — they're defeated. The same thing happened in Upper Canada — Ontario. The petit-bourgeoisie under William Lyon Mackenzie tried to lead the bourgeois-democratic revolution against the British and they, too, were defeated.

Both the Patriotes and the Patriots, as they were called, fought bravely in those Revolutions of 1837-39 but they couldn't win because the material conditions hadn't developed yet.

The Québécois Emerge

The Canayens were more than ever outlaws. They had dared revolt against Queen Victoria???!!! They must be wiped out! Lord Durham thought it could be done quite simply by assimilation. Outlaws, uncivilized, bloody savages who don't speak properly, they must be made into within-laws, proper civilized uptight English Protestants, good proletarians working for the English bourgeoisie.

But outlaws don't disappear just like that. They're thick-skinned, they resist. Despite the union of Upper and Lower Canada, despite English-speaking immigration, despite Confederation which locks them into a reserve, the Canayens just won't disappear. Some leave for the States to find jobs. Others go to Manitoba and Saskatchewan to homestead. The ones who stay in Quebec bow and scrape under the clerical order, which becomes stronger than ever. The bishops, more Catholic than the Pope, launch a regime of seminary schooling, at the same time as capitalist industry makes its appearance, looking for good, disciplined workers.

Then, the first half of this century, things seemed to be working in this land of Quebec. Priests, brothers, sisters were being churned out en masse. Our main export! People moving from the country to the city to find jobs in factories. The outlaw tamed. A good boy who knew his place and stayed there. Mr. Nobody, Mr. Invisible, Mr. Excuse-me-for-living. You'd think he'd forgotten he was a Canayen, except maybe on St-Jean-Baptiste Day.

Born for crumbs. Morning prayers, evening prayers, Sunday Mass, Easter, the first Friday of the month, rosaries, confessions, the whole bundle. We were sheep, but Lord were we bad. We swore, we drank, we told dirty stories, we spoke French, we spoke bad English too. We were on our knees but it wasn't enough, we had to *crawl* goddammit!

Then in the '60s, bang! He didn't call himself Canayen any more; he was now a *Québécois.* He began by feeling he belonged to a people. Québécois meant something dammit. He saw he was caught in a structure of exploitation. One, two. As a people, colonized; as workers, exploited. Just like that. A double-barreled shotgun. Bang, bang.

I bet a generation from now we'll be rid of the Vatican. People aren't taken in anymore. Getting out of the *habit* y'could say! There's so many cassocks being tossed in the bushes, the bushes're covered up from the good Lord's sun! Then there're the nuns who get dressed up in ordinary clothes. You can't tell them apart anymore. Pretty soon you'll marry one and then after the third kid she'll tell you she's a nun. What a hell of a joke *that'd* be on the guy!

What about the capitalist order? Do you think it'll last much longer?

Not bloody likely!

The English, the Americans, *they've* digested capitalism, even the workers because they could always identify with their bourgeoisie who belong to the same ethnic group. And they know what side their bread is buttered on.

Come on now, we got bourgeois.

Yes, we have bourgeois, but not a bourgeoisie as such. That is, we don't have an owning class of bourgeois that concentrates capital and controls a good part of our nation's economy.

That's true.

We do have a bourgeoisie whose capital is tied in with the Canadian and American concentrations of capital. But even these guys, I dunno but you'd think they weren't real capitalists. Oh, I'm not talking about Paul Desmarias[1] — he's a real sellout all right. But there are lots of others. They are capitalists, but there's always something of the Canayen in them that keeps bugging them.

We're All Communists

In the present system, succeeding means putting yourself in a position superior to others and exploiting them. But we're always knocking the guy who tries to get ahead. Either we all rise or nobody rises.

That's communistic!

1 Quebec's E.P. Taylor, President of Power Corporation which owns six newspapers, four radio stations, Consolidated Bathurst.

That's right. Basically we're all communists.

Don't tell my mother that!

We'd much rather work together than compete with each other. Oh, I'm not talking about those who try to assimilate as best they can the capitalist system, with its competition, its profits and its private property. No. I'm talking about real people, ordinary people, ordinary Québécois, workers. Look what used to happen in the countryside. Wasn't that cooperation, communism?

A farmer would build his stable and everyone around would help him. His farm would burn to the ground and a month later he'd have a brand new house and stable and pigpen, without it costing him a cent. And it wasn't by insurance. There was no insurance then. Or rather, there was *real* insurance. The insurance that if some misfortune happened to you, everyone around would help you. That's what you have in China. We're communists, I tell you. Even if they've tried to make capitalists out of us. And then, the joie de vivre, the whole gang having fun together, having big parties with the family, the neighbours, everybody, cutting loose, what's that?

It ain't communist!

It bloody well *is* communist! As communist as you can get.

Well, capitalists have fun, too.

Yes, but not the same way. Take a look at our own aspiring capitalists. Ever been to a bourgeois party? First of all, they're all dressed up, trying to make an impression. Constipated, with the little woman looking like a walking Christmas tree. They start talking business with the first drink — how much money they made, how they screwed a guy — and they think that's funny. And all this time they're watching each other, to see who's on the way up, who's going down. Christ, bullshit like you wouldn't believe! And out of the corner of their eye, they're watching the women, to see if there isn't one they can grab in a corner of the house. They're watching themselves, checking themselves to be sure they're impressing those they're supposed to impress. Alcohol loosens them up a bit, notch by notch. But what comes out isn't spontaneous, isn't fun, isn't honest fellowship. It's vinegar, frustration, vomit, bitterness, guilty conscience over being doublecrossers, hatred for people. And when they get their pants down, well, there's a little dicky, aching from a bladder overfilled with whisky.

Come on, you're making me sick!

Not to mention their poor Christmas-tree wives . . .

Never mind, I get the picture.

When a bourgeois has fun, he pisses vinegar. It stands to reason. If you doublecross people, you can't love people. To have fun with people, you have to love people. Loving is certainly not doublecrossing. It's giving, sharing, accepting a gift without being suspicious, giving other people a chance, giving them the benefit of the doubt, relaxing, knowing how to relax with other people. How can you relax when you spend your days robbing other people, cheating them, pulling the rug out from under them? Impossible.

But what about the real rich ones with their big yachts . . .?

Just look at their faces. Where's the serenity? Not to mention the joy. All tensed up for Chrissake. It's nerve-racking, keeping an eye on fortunes like those. Especially as there are all those people you've robbed who'd like to get back what's theirs. Those nice smiles are just for the newsmen.

If we take off our capitalist overcoat, we'll find a bunch of communists underneath?

Yes. Even Real Caouette. Even that petit-bourgeois Caouette who sells American cars for a living. Scratch the surface a bit and you'll find a communist.

Impossible!

Well, maybe I am exaggerating. Caouette's too far gone. But most Créditistes are communists who don't know it.

Jeez, don't tell *them* that, they'll kill you!

They are rural people, uprooted farmers, small businessmen. Industrial society has rolled over them like a steamroller. That's why they rant and rave about high finance and the big trusts. They're against imperialism, the capitalism that we know today. Caouette was the only party leader to talk about U.S. control of Canada in the 1974 federal election. Creditistes are anti-capitalists but also reactionary, because they want to return to the way of production of the past. They're still dreaming of the pre-capitalist system of small merchant production, which goes back to the 17th century, when everyone had his little business. The farmer, the baker, the grocer, the blacksmith, all exchanged goods and services with everyone else. This explains their moral and religious stances too. But seeing as you can't turn back the clock they'll be moving forward to the next historical stage with the rest of us. They're going to have to orient themselves towards socialism.

Communist créditistes! I'll believe it when I see it!

Mercier, Duplessis, Levesque

To get back to nationalism . . .

Yeah, let's . . .

After the Revolutions of 1837-39 the clerics tried to regain their stranglehold on Quebec patriotism. Being a patriot meant being an infantryman defending the secular interests of the Pope, being a patriot meant following the Catholic religion.

Yeah, but we supported Louis Riel.

When Riel was executed in Regina, thousands of Canayens protested against Ottawa and the Church who were in league against the métis chief. Riel was a hero of Quebec. But right away there were politicians who turned this wave of patriotism to their advantage. Laurier of course. And Honoré Mercier, who in 1886 founded the *national party* "to liberate Quebec." What did we get? Big daddy Mercier elected premier thanks to the patriotism of Canayens, caught with his hand in the cookie jar.[1] Bought off, sold out, rotten in less than ten years.

The disappointment our grandfathers had! Give a guy a chance to get us out of the shit, and he buggers off with the shovel . . .

---

1 It seems he had taken a $100,000 bribe from the contractors who were building the Baie des Chaleurs railway!

Duplessis (right) with Camilien Houde. Houde was elected Mayor of Montreal in 1930, and gave up his place as leader of the provincial Conservatives to Duplessis. The Duplessis regime was one of severe repression for the Québécois.

So the Liberals were returned to power in Quebec and they went on giving the country away to the Americans . . .

. . . until a new reformer came along in the '30s to save Quebec . . . Maurice Duplessis.

That's right. The Depression brought a new wave of social protest. The Québécois were disgusted with government corruption and the failure of the capitalist system. Duplessis proclaimed himself the new Messiah who would clean up the province of Quebec, free it from the grip of the Americans, and make it a livable land for the Québécois. But still within Confederation of course. Self-determination Duplessis-style.

But good old Maurice became the Yankee capitalists' best friend.

His self-determination meant being able to deal directly with Washington without having to go through the middlemen in Ottawa.

His job was keeping things quiet in Quebec. Sending the provincial police in to beat up striking workers.

Persecuting those who were for social progress. Duplessis the reformer became Duplessis the reactionary.

And then the Liberals again in the '60s.

The new clerics, Lesage's fair-haired boys, modernizing Quebec, bringing it into the Atomic Age, integrating it more completely into American continentalism.

But they gave impetus to a new wave of nationalism. We wanted to be modern. We wanted to re-enter the world after the dark Duplessis years. But we wanted to do it as Québécois. The contradiction blew up in Lesage's face, and he disappeared into the business pages of La Presse.

The two aspects of the contradiction today are found on one hand in Bourassa, with his Liberal tradition of *roinègre* for the Americans, and on the other hand in Lévesque with the revival of nationalism. René Lévesque is Honoré Mercier of 1886, Duplessis of 1936. The wave of patriotism is mounting. "Rally round the party that will liberate us — vote *Parti National*, sorry I mean *Union Nationale*, I mean *Parti Québécois!*"

Yeah, but René's a good guy.

Sure he's a good guy. A guy's sincerity is important, no doubt about that. His personal merit. But those are his subjective qualities, what he's like as a person. What's more important is how *he* sees the objective world. You can have a nice guy everybody likes for all sorts of reasons, but what I'm interested in is how he reacts when you take him into the lunch-bucket neighbourhoods. If he counts votes, he's a double-crosser no matter what party he's from, Liberal, Union Nationale, Parti Québécois. If he thinks it's a shame, something must be done to help these poor people, he's a social democrat, a guy with a guilty conscience, a guy who in the final analysis will do nothing for these people once he's in power. But if he sees these people as the oppressed who must organize to overthrow the gang of exploiters, then I'd begin to respect him.

In other words, for you, the guy has to recognize the class struggle, and become part of the exploited class to change things.

It's absolutely necessary. However, the *Parti Québécois* and its leadership absolutely abhors the class struggle. They recognize social classes all right, but they want to sweep the class struggle under the carpet of the "Quebec community". "Everyone come join the party; workers, bourgeois, petit-bourgeois, we're Québécois one and all! Once inside we must bury our differences in order to attain what will give all of us power — independence."

PART III

Economic Struggle,
the Unions

The State, a Tool of the Bourgeoisie

But independence *is* a necessary stage. After that we can see.

Whoa. *That* is nationalist evangelism! "Let's all walk hand in hand, exploiters and exploited, towards the promised land of independence. Once we're there we'll see." Not for me, thanks.

Okay, smart guy.

We have to explain some things. The best way to begin would be to go back to our structures . . . Society is structured.

Right.

The structure is authoritarian.

Right.

The economic structure determines the political structure.

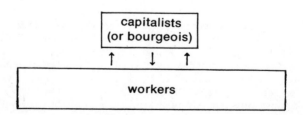

Right.

The economic structure we have is that of a minority exploiting a majority.

There is no harmony between these two groups. One produces but doesn't own the product. The other doesn't produce but owns the product. That, creates a conflict. Agreed?

Agreed.

These two groups are called 'social classes.'

Right.

The bourgeois class, bankers, factory owners, transport owners, wishes to consolidate its assets and accumulate even more. On the other hand, the working class, possessing only its labour power, must sell it for as much as possible. Until such time as it can overthrow the bourgeoisie and become owner of the goods it produces by taking over the means of production, the factories, and the resources. This conflict is the fundamental contradiction in capitalist society. It's the conflict that is at the root of all political, social, racial, cultural, and ecological problems . . .

Hold on!

If that contradiction is resolved, old buddy, the other problems will be small potatoes.

You can see the workers taking over their shops . . .

Yes.

Oh yeah!

Not so fast. To keep workers in their place the bourgeois have to organise a whole side show. Without that . . .

The workers would throw those bastards out real fast.

The sideshow is the State.

The government?

Yes. But what is behind that side show is what we call political power. Authority. With the power of life and death over its subjects.

Life and death?

Public Archives of Canada

Police with machine guns line up awaiting orders in Iroquois Club lobby during Asbestos Strike 1949. The asbestos miners fought a long battle against the Duplessis' repressive forces and won.

Yes.

How is that?

People have been hung in Canada, electrocuted in the United States, guillotined in France. Today it's a life sentence. A form of death.

Yes, but that's justice.

Hold on! What was that again?

That's social order.

Whose order?

The government's.

That's what I'm telling you. State order.

Yes, but in a democracy the State . . .

Does it belong to you?

No.

Not to me either.

Not to anybody. The State mustn't belong to anybody. It must be above everybody. So's it can govern better and be fairer with everybody. The State is above social classes.

That'll be the day!

Well, that's what it looks like to me.

Well, that's just what they *want* you to think, that the State is above everybody, to pull the wool over your eyes. Are we governed by men or by gods?

By men.

If we're governed by men, they're in the same boat as you and me. There's nothing special about them. So how come you're giving them the power that people used to give the gods?

Well, their power comes from God.

Hey, you believe *that*?

Well, that's what they told me.

If it comes from God, it can't come from the people. Your democracy sounds more like a theocracy!

Listen, I never thought it came from the good Lord, okay? Never mind where it comes from, you still need authority.

Authority and Leadership

You and me and a bunch of people are on an island. Do we need authority to tell us what to do and what not to do?

Well, it depends.

Agreed. But what does it depend on? First of all, there's a distinction to be made between leadership and authority. Authority imposes its will indiscriminately to defend interests which are not those of the people. Leadership is the vanguard of a group which is struggling for its own interests. For example, in the white society of New France, authority was embodied in the governor, the intendent, and the bishop. These three musketeers imposed (or tried to impose) the feudal law of the king of France on the Canayens. A few miles away, in an Iroquois camp, the chief of the tribe was *not* an authority but a leader. The chief never imposed his own will. And more important still, he never represented special interests, either his own or those of the chiefs as a group. He defended the interests of the whole tribe. The chief was the one who was most aware of the common good of the whole tribe, and who at the same time was ready to do everything he could for its survival and development. He was a leader. You see the difference?

Nope. Was the chief a boss or wasn't he?

The chief wasn't a boss. He always consulted all the members of the tribe in council meetings on all decisions touching on the welfare of the tribe. He gave his opinion like everyone else. His opinion might carry more weight, because he could see the situation more clearly. But he never thought of packing the council or making backroom deals to swindle people and accumulate wealth for his gang or his family. You can see it's altogether different.

You mean the leader is the best man of the whole tribe, who works the hardest for the tribe, while the authority is the doublecrosser, who sets up his deals to make it look like he's working for everybody when actually he's just working for his own gang.

Yes.

But what authority do that gang of bourgeois have?

The State. That's the trick. To defend their class interests, they use the authority conferred on the State which seems to be above everybody.

But what we have in fact is this:

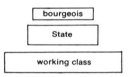

The State, the Authority in our society, is a tool in the hands of the bourgeoisie to keep the workers working for them.

A tool? Civil authority a tool?

A tool.

Like a machine?

Yes, a machine to protect the interests of the bourgeoisie by locking the workers into a regime of capitalist exploitation.

How the Bourgeoisie Does Things

Let's say you're a bourgeois.

Lay off the insults, will ya?!

Let's say you have a million bucks . . .

I'd have it spent in a month. First, I'd trade the old bus in on a new Chrysler, I'd buy the wife a nice coat . . .

It's clear, you're no bourgeois.

But the guys'd say I was, with the Chrysler. I'd have to

move to Outremont!

That wouldn't make you a bourgeois. They don't spend money like that.

Come on. What about their yachts and their cottages?

No. That's just small change. A bourgeois is someone who first of all, invests his money to get a return on it. Okay? His profit is divided in two, one part is reinvested, the other part he uses to live. The proportion between the two depends on what his ambitions are. If he is building a financial or industrial empire, he'll spend hardly any more than you do. He'll wear the same suit four or five years, he won't tip, he won't spend a dime in a nightclub. His children will have only the strict necessities and will quickly learn to economise. But as his investments grow, he'll allow himself a few more expenses, but never foolish spending — well calculated expenses — what he needs to live comfortably, what he needs to impress the workers and the other bourgeois, and that's all. Everything CALCULATED.

But there are bourgeois who live the high life.

You do have upstarts, who have just made their first million, and not having the bourgeois virtues of thrift, sobriety, and planning, burn it up in a year. How many French-Canadians do that?

Then there are the petit-bourgeois of one ethnic group who want to show the bourgeoisie of another ethnic group that they've made it. Jewish, Italian, and French-Canadian upstarts in Montreal driving around Westmount in canary-yellow Jags . . .

But let's say you're an established bourgeois. You have a million in profits this year. You want to reinvest it. You use your business contacts to find out where this million can bring you the best return. It's normal — the law of capital. It's the law of the bourgeoisie.

Let's say you find out through your contacts at the Club Richelieu of Ste-Thérèse, that you belong to, that there's a lot of money in manufacturing antique furniture. There are lots of Québécois and Americans who want to furnish their homes with old chests or 18th century Canadian cupboards. And *you* are going to satisfy the demand. There's another bourgeois at the club with money to invest. Good. The next day, you talk it over at the office. Building a factory, finding workers. Land is very reasonable in the industrial park in St-Jérôme, because the mayor wants to "develop" the town. There's even a reduction in municipal taxes, especially to "attract industry."

For a couple of hundred bucks, you incorporate. "Antiquités Ti-Jos Marleau Antiques Inc." There are large numbers of unemployed in St-Jérôme; there must be some good woodworkers in the bunch. You have a good contact in the lumber industry. You buy modern machinery. And then off you go. Six months later, your first 1812 pine chests come off the assembly line. Your salesman has already gotten orders from the *King of Furniture* for all his stores. Your workers are working hard, sales are good, the mayor of St-Jérôme is happy.

And also, the government hasn't bothered you. It's collected excise tax, which annoys you a bit, but after all you're ready to do your part to help the government maintain public order, to keep in business.

In the morning you look at yourself in the mirror, and you like what you see. Thanks to you, men are working. Their children have food to eat. Thanks to you, the country is developing. Québec is moving ahead. You're a somebody. You have the feeling you're indispensable. At least to hundreds of people. A little shiver runs up and down your spine. You don't know exactly what it is, but you like it. It tickles. It's a bit indecent, because it's a feeling that can't be shared. You never talk about it, not even to your wife. She wouldn't understand. A sweet solitary sin.

It's the feeling of power. The feeling that you can exercise power over the lives of hundreds of people. Domination. And it's so pleasing to you, that you prefer it to all other pleasures, alcohol, sex, or travel. If you had to choose you'd drop all the others before you'd drop that one. You're a boss. You're a bourgeois.

You're making me sick.

But your workers are starting to look at you differently. You still call them by their first names, pat them on the back as you walk by, smile your best smile. But they're not the same, they're wary of you. You panic. You call in your foreman. He isn't able to tell you anything, except that things aren't going too well in the shop.

You, who gave them their jobs, gave them their daily bread — what could those heartless wretches have against you? You spy on them. You send your secretary as a decoy, to see what's going on. Then one day you find out. A cancer in the shop. Your workers want a union. You hit the roof. You want to kill them all. Those rotten, ungrateful sons of bitches, goddam shits, good-for-nothings that you lifted out of the gutter, they're all against you, plotting to rob you of your possessions you sweated so hard for.

Let me go on. *I'm* the boss in your story, eh?!

Go right ahead.

Well now, I toss them all out and hire new ones.

Then six months later, the new ones want a union. What do you do then?

I says to myself, if these guys want a union so bad, I'll set one up myself. That way, it'll be on my side from the start.

So you form your company union.

That's right. My company union looks after good public relations between me and my workers — Christmas bonuses, a Christmas tree for the kiddies, parties for the wives once a year, a picnic every August.

Sounds like you know all about it.

We had a union like that at the shop for two years before we got a real one. So I know the story. Two or three guys start barfing on the boss's Christmas cake. They start criticizing, mouthing off. One of them gets fired. The other two get a few more together and meet to form a real union. Now *that* was hard work, convincing the other workers we needed a real fighting union so's we could all get decent wages, and working conditions we could put up with.

But what about the boss?

The boss could go screw himself.

Now you're taking the worker's point of view . . .

Hell, you be the boss now. I can't do it no more, it's too disgusting.

I get the dirty work, eh?

It's your story? So you do the dirty work.

All right. So I'm the boss and I'm biting my nails.

And I'm the worker and I'm rubbing my hands.

We're gonna get you, you bastard! If you think you're gonna exploit us much longer, decide who works, when we work, what we work at, what working conditions we have, well you're wrong, buddy. So then we sign up members for the Ti-Jos Marleau Employees Union. But there are some guys who're scared.

That's because I terrorize them. If they sign up, they're fired.

They'll tell you they're not signing up, but they do, and our union asks the government for certification.

If the government gives you the right to operate in my factory, that means the government's on your side.

Are you nuts?

Well let's see. There's nothing more opposed to the bosses than unions.

Are you putting me on?

Listen. I've got the boss's job and I'm defending myself.

You wanna know something? It took a hundred years of workers' struggles to obtain the right to unionize. And if the government recognizes that right today, it's not because it's a government by the workers for the workers. It's still a government of the bosses, but it's had to give ground and tolerate the existence of unions, otherwise there'd be a real uproar.

Still, it's not my government, if they do that to me.

Oh yes, it's still your government. Just because we got a union don't mean you're not boss any more.

The union's not a bad thing for you. All it keeps you from doing is following your whims, firing someone 'cause you don't like his mug, or giving a girl a promotion if she lets you grab her ass.

Am I or am I not the boss? Is it or is it not my factory?

It's *my* money I put into it. It's mine so I'm entitled to do what I want.

Listen, boss! You employ *people* to work, yes or no?

Yes.

Well, people are people. They're entitled to at least some rights. All the union does is keep you from acting like a pig.

It's the workers who should obey the boss. I demand a vote on the union. You're not going to railroad me like that.

Okay, you'll get a vote, then you'll see.

So then *I* put pressure on the fencesitters so that they vote against the union.

That won't get you anywhere. The guys'll stick together. Your company union is replaced by a real union, and in no time at all you have to negotiate a collective agreement. You won't have any part of it, so after the required waiting period a strike is called.

The Strike at Ti-Jos Marleau's

Then I feel like killing you all.

Pickets are set up around the factory. You're the only one we let in.

Well I want my factory to produce, so I hire other workers.

Yeah, SCABS!

Well *they're* ready to work.

They're unemployed workers who have to cross a picket line to earn a living. But we don't let them through.

Intimidation! Threats! Violence!

Our right to strike is also the right to stop production.

Not a chance! The goddam government'll do *something* for me, for Chrissake!

Come on, bosses don't swear like workers!

An angry boss is entitled to swear all he wants — as long as there are no ladies around. So then, my lawyers apply

Strikers stop trucks as police try to bring scabs through picket line at Dominion Textile Strike, Montreal 1946. Viciously anti-union employers could readily get police help in strike-breaking.

for an injunction against the strikers.

So the judges, who are already on your side, grant it to you.

No more than three pickets in front of the factory. Three lousy strikers aren't going to keep my new workers out.

Dirty lowdown pig! There you proved the government's on your side. You get an injunction and you got cops watching the factory, too. We got to use other means.

Window-breakers! Vandals! Terrorists!

We'll make your scabs understand that it's unhealthy to cross a picket line. And then the trucks that come in, they don't come back again.

Faced with your bandit tactics, I have no choice but to use the same means. I hire men . . .

Guys from the underworld, you mean.

Never mind where they come from. They're going to protect my property against you thugs.

Let's not forget the papers and the TV. It'll be on the CBC news. They'll make us out to be firebugs, bullies . . .

. . . which you are.

So we distribute leaflets explaining our position, and organise a demonstration in St-Jérôme. The police rough us up a bit. It hits the papers again, all the media against us.

Bunch of socialist communist anarchist unionists! All you want is disorder, discord, conflict, struggle, resentment, confusion, misfortune for the workers, misfortune for the bosses, calamity!

After two months with only fifteen or twenty bucks a week from the strike fund, we start getting a bit depressed.

Yes, but think how it is for me, with all the money I've lost. A quarter of a million. The longer it lasts, the more I lose. I let you know, through the newspapers, that if you don't yield, I'll close up shop.

That don't scare us.

That was my trump card. I swallow my pride. I'm ready

to negotiate. I have to speak to workers on an equal basis. You don't know how humiliating that is.

You end up granting us more or less decent working conditions, reasonable wages. We shake hands, the strike is over, we go back to work.

The Class Nature of the Trade Union Struggle

So you see, I didn't get the impression, as a boss, that the government was on my side.

It sure wasn't on the side of the workers.

You see that we both had the feeling that the government was on the other side.

That's true.

So what side *was* it on?

It wasn't on the side of the boss, but over him, an arbitrator as I was saying before.

No.

What do you mean, no?

It was just on the side of the boss. Your strike didn't threaten the structure of exploitation at all. It was aimed at improving working conditions. The bosses' government isn't opposed to workers having better wages so they can eat properly so that they can work better. At first glance, it hurts the boss who gets it, but in fact if he thinks it over some more, he will see that his loss will benefit his class as a whole. The wage increases will be spent buying goods and services, yielding profits to other bourgeois. In fact, strikes improve the workers' situation temporarily but at the same time they bind them all the more closely to the boss. It is the best of all possible worlds — bourgeois worlds, that is.

There's been a quantitative change, but not a qualitative one. The boss is still the boss, the one who makes all the decisions, and he remains the owner of the shop. It's when you attack these relationships that you find out for real that the government is a special device in the hands of the bourgeoisie. Just try laying your hands on the shop, and watch things get hot.

Okay. I'm imagining that at Antiquités Ti-Jos Marleau Antiques us workers don't really need bosses, like you say. What do we do then?

You tell me.

One morning, the whole bunch of us go into the boss's office and stand around him, real nice. We tell him we think his enterprise belongs to us, we're the real producers, etc., the whole story you were just telling me. Okay, boss, what're you gonna do now?

I keep my cool. Put my hand on the phone.

One of the guys cut the wire on the way in.

That's unlawful confinement! Occupation! A kidnapping!

We want to talk to you.

My dear friends, you work for me. You're supposed to be working right now. Would you be so good as to leave my office immediately and go back to your machines. It is stipulated in the collective agreement signed by your union and by me that . . .

Shaddup!

Is this a revolt? A revolution?

It's just that we want to tell you something. We're going to be frank about it. The factory is ours. Your work is just organizing us. We're not dumdums, we're able to organize ourselves, by ourselves. We're big boys now. You're going to draw up a paper that says the workers of the factory are the owners. You too, if you like. If you want to stay on as administrative advisor.

That is absolute insanity! It's abominable! Why, I've never seen such impudence!

We're talking to you, goddammit!

Gentlemen, I'll have you know that what you are doing is a criminal act. The courts call this act unlawful confinement. This act, as serious as kidnapping, could bring you fifteen years in prison, minimum. It's your choice. Clear the premises immediately and I won't press any charges.

Keep it up and the full force of the law will be brought to bear on you.

Christ! Hey, we ain't doing too well, are we? Yeah, that makes the guys stop and think.

You see? You want to change relationships. You don't want any boss anymore. The means you've just used could lead to fifteen years behind bars. What side is the state apparatus on?

But there's no other way. We know ahead of time asking him nicely ain't going to get him to hand over the company.

And you won't get it by buying him out either. If business is good, he won't sell. If business is bad, you won't buy it. Even if business is good, you can't buy it with the money you make, or without mortgaging your labour until the day you die and for two or three generations after you.

Listen, if the factory belongs to us, we wouldn't be crazy enough to buy it. Buying it is out of the question. It's ours, we're taking it.

How?

To start with, we go back to work, to think it over.

There, you see, you're not just asking for 10c more an hour any more. You are touching the private property of the means of production, the cornerstone of the capitalist system. And there, old man, you're striking at the heart. Everything will be put into operation to keep the workers from taking over the means of production, the factories, the means of transportation, the whole business.

First they'll use the law — their law. The judges, the police, the whole prison system. And if your activities spread, they use the army, emergency legislation, the War Measures Act, concentration camps, extradition trials. All perfectly legal. The State passing the legislation it needs to maintain the system of capitalist exploitation, but doing it in the name of the people, for the common good, to preserve Law and Order, to serve Justice, for the happiness of all, and all that bullshit.

Are you trying to scare me?

No, I'm just telling you how the setup works.

Meaning us guys at Ti-Jos Marleau Antiques can go on strike all we want and win our demands without hurting anyone, but soon as we decide to take over the shop, then the shit hits the fan.

All right, confine the boss, have him sign a "new testament." What do you do after that?

We make him sign a piece of paper saying he won't sue us.

You can wipe your ass with that piece of paper. Legally it's absolutely worthless.

We tell him if he sues us, we'll break his legs.

The law comes down very heavily on people who threaten bosses.

You mean we got no way to hold him?

No, and as soon as you let him go, he'll charge you, and the system will crush you.

At least we'll still be standing up dammit!

Political Struggle,
a Workers' Party

The General Strike, May 1972

If there were a way you could be more effective . . .

Yeah, I see what you're getting at. It can't only happen at Ti-Jos Marleau's. We got to take action. But it's got to happen other places too.

That's it. People will talk about your action. Other workers will understand that it's the only possible way.

So we contact other workers through the union and the union centres. We force the CSN(CNTU)[1] into taking more radical positions. The FTQ (Quebec Federation of Labour)[2] joins in. Teachers realise they're not professionals, just working people . . .

Aren't we just going over the union history of these last few years?

Of course. A common front of the CSN, the FTQ, and the CEQ (Quebec Teachers Corportion)[3] is being formed. When the contract of government, hospital, and school employees — what we call the public sector — comes up for negotiation, these three federations will be negotiating directly with the government.

With the State employer, that is. There, the apparatus of

1 The CNTU represents 150,000 workers
2 The QFL represents 200,000 workers
3 The CEQ represents 70,000 teachers

La Presse

Demonstrators march down St. Catharine Street, Montreal, to occupy the studios of radio station CKAC during the General Strike, May 1972.

repression itself is the boss. Watch out!

Injunctions are issued. The workers defy them.

So there are a hundred union members in prison, with their three leaders Pepin, Laberge, and Charbonneau.[1]

But the workers don't get intimidated. On the contrary, there are walkouts all across the province. Workers occupy the town of Sept-Îles. Thetford Mines, too. It's nearly a general strike. All sectors are affected. Workers are occupying radio and TV stations.

Instead of just sitting on their asses, they went into action. Taking over the means of communication, keeping their workshops operating without the bosses, as they did at the Albert Prévost Institute. Now *that,* old man, is a revolution in progress.

Yeah, but after six or seven days the bosses sent the police to get those guys out, at Albert Prévost.

Yes, but why? Things were going well. The hospital was working better than it was when the bosses were there.

All of a sudden, there was no more oppression by hospital authorities. The authoritarian framework was gone. The doctors had freedom in their work. The workers did their work because they were really participating in the operation of the place, helping to cure the patients. The patients had never had better care. There were even some who could see themselves recovering for the first time.

It couldn't last. It was absolutely necessary to nip this revolution in the bud. Can you picture a psychiatric institution starting to cure its patients?! It loses its *raison d'etre.* Its role is to perpetuate itself as an institution, by keeping the sick, sick as long as possible.

But what was most intolerable for the administrators was the proof that they were dispensable, that the workers could run such a place without them. That was really an attack on the system. This revolutionary movement had to be broken. They couldn't let cleaning ladies participate in administrative decisions, couldn't let an orderly know why he was treating a patient as he was. They particularly had

---

1 Leaders of the CNTU, QFL, CEQ jailed after defying Bourassa's injunction during the General Strike, 1972.

to re-establish the authoritarian, oppressive framework of bourgeois dictatorship.

And they did it in half an hour. The anti-riot squad came in, and right after that the administrators went back into their offices and re-established their authority.

Yeah, and a bloody shame, too.

Those guys did what they could, but they could of resisted a bit more.

What for? For the glory? For their honour?

Come on, don't talk crap. Only a nut would enjoy getting his head knocked in. You have to know when to make strategic retreats. Faced with superior forces, you have to know when to withdraw. Being stubborn and running at a brick wall with your head down is just a good way to crack your skull open. It's just burning up your strength and playing into the hands of your opponent, handing over your troops on a silver platter. It's just pulling a François the First, who said after a defeat that all was lost save honour. That's okay for a feudal king. But for someone who wants to change a regime, you don't get very far with honour.

You shouldn't be scared of a fight.

If you spend your time looking for fights to prove to yourself and others that you're not afraid, you're all screwed up. You'll get beaten up.

Well okay, but then there's nothing we can do. They'll clean us out everywhere we turn.

All right. Here comes *the* question. What do we do? The workers can occupy work sites and keep them operating. But they don't have at hand the means to defend what they've succeeded in taking.

It's *rifles* we need, by Jesus!

You grab your rifle, they bring out their tanks, bazookas, mortars, armoured helicopters —

Okay, okay!

Seizing the State Apparatus

The first front was the struggle at your place of work, trying to gain ground in the economic organization of your work. But you can't go any farther right away, because of the repressive force of the bourgeois State. You now have to open up a second front. The political front. You have to take over the State.

Oh yeah, just like that! You're a real joker, you bastard.

I didn't say "just like that". I said that's what you had to do. How to do it is another matter.

Yeah.

You see, there already are workers who have had the experience of economic struggle carried to its limit. The results, overall, aren't inspiring. Take the Spanish workers who waged a fantastic economic struggle from 1931 to 1936. While certain more or less radical parties were battling in parliament with the liberal and rightist parties, the workers were taking over factories and large farms, and organizing them on the principle of self-management or workers' co-operatives. They were making a revolution in their places of work. No more large landowners, no more capitalist bosses. They reorganized the economy on socialist principles. But they didn't advance their struggle on the political front. Maybe they were hoping that the political parties would do enough shouting at each other in the House to lose their voices, and then quietly wither away, along with the government, and the whole state apparatus.

Well they didn't. Especially not the army. And it was within the army that the struggle against the workers began. A certain little colonel named Franco gathered around him all the anti-worker elements, the dispossessed landlords, the expropriated factory owners, and as always the Church. So then that goddam fascist Franco, with the help of Hitler and Mussolini, began the "cleanup" of Spain, what we call the Spanish Civil War of 1936-39. The workers also started to organize for the fight . . .

Okay, I understand. Franco seizes the State apparatus, the police, the army. He becomes the Authority who's going to restore Social Order and massacre workers.

That's not bad, in a nutshell. Anyway, we're not going to reenact the Spanish Civil War. It's a matter of understanding that we must seize the state apparatus, the government, and all its authority, so that we can continue to change social relationships. If not, watch out!

The PQ is not a Socialist Party

Okay. So we have to go into politics.

But not politics the way the oldline parties do it. Not politicking. No political games like that bunch of puppets. Winning elections to fill their pockets, hand out patronage — stunts the Liberals and the Union Nationale have been pulling for generations. To take hold of the State, we need a party. A party which will wage the struggle on the political front properly speaking.

There's the Parti Québécois.

That's a political party all right, but it's not a workers' party.

Seems there's quite a few workers in it.

That still doesn't make it a workers' party.

It's the working-class districts that elected Parti Québécois MPs.

That still doesn't make it a workers' party.

Okay wiseguy, what *is* a workers' party anyway?

A workers' party wishes to change the structures of exploitation we were just talking about.

That's what you call a socialist party.

A real socialist party, yes. The PQ isn't a socialist party.

But it does want change.

Change what?

First, it wants Québec to separate from Canada.

That's fine. It stands to reason that a people like the Québécois should be freed from the political domination of another people. Where we have at present one federal state, with the separation of Quebec there would be a federal state (the rest of Canada) and a unitary state (Quebec). It would be a rearrangement of states, but it wouldn't change the internal structure of either state in any way.

Well, isn't that something? You'd think to hear you, you

were opposed.

Just because I think it's not enough doesn't mean I'm opposed.

Well, for a diehard independentist, you sure sound like it.

Maybe, to someone who sees only independence, like some great day of glory. I'm for independence all the way, but I'm also for the changing of structures, all the way.

So you mean the PQ just wants independence, the realignment of the Canadian State into two states. Nothing else.

You tell me what else they want.

They want to "civilise capital."

What does *that* mean?

It means the companies should think more about people and less about their profits.

How do you make them do that?

The PQ says we'll see once we have independence, once we have the tools in hand.

What tools?

Our independence.

Independence is a tool? How?

We get back from Ottawa the powers we should have.

The powers of a State?

That's right, the powers of a sovereign State.

So the powers of State are a tool?

Yes, you see, the PQ agrees — the State is a tool, an apparatus.

Fine. We agree up to that point. But a while ago we agreed that the State is a special apparatus for repression, and that at present in Quebec, as in all capitalist countries, this special apparatus for repression is in the hands of the bourgeois, yes or no?

Yes.

So, what happens if the PQ is elected? Does this special apparatus for repression stay in the hands of the bourgeois or not?

Well . . . I dunno.

That's important, seems to me.

Well, the PQ says it will be the State of all Québécois, big and small, the State of all Quebec's social classes, bourgeois and worker, unemployed and people on welfare, widows and orphans. Québec for all Québécois.

Trudeau says that Canada is for all Canadians, for all the social classes in Canada, that his job is to see to the equilibrium between different classes and different groups. And Trudeau is the perfect prime minister for a bourgeois State.

So you mean if we transpose all that to Quebec, after independence, the PQ will do just what Trudeau does in Ottawa — try to keep the equilibrium between bosses and workers?

Yes, but in some ways they'll have an easier time of it. They'll have the nationalists all sewed up.

I don't get it.

There is currently a nationalist movement in Quebec, is there not?

Yes.

The PQ currently monopolizes the nationalist feeling and the nationalist movement in Quebec, does it not?

Yes.

You can be a bourgeois, a worker, on welfare, from any social class, right or left, extreme right or centre. If you're a Québécois nationalist, you can join the PQ, right?

Right.

The only criterion is that you reject federalism and give your allegiance to Quebec.

Yes.

If you're a "real Québécois" as they say, you cannot be opposed to the PQ.

That's what it looks like.

In the big happy Québécois family of the PQ, you find the same class structures as in the oldline parties, "Québécois, love one another, exploiting boss or unemployed, Outremont society matron or east-end cleaning lady, we are all Qué-bé-cois." The magic word. Zap! The Great Reconciliation of all classes — just say the magic word. Three syllables and it's done. With two fingers raised in a V — the peace sign, just as if the exploitation of workers was only in the head, like a bad dream. Workers kiss bosses, because they are all Québécois.

Well, now, them there kissing parties ain't going to help the workers' struggle.

Not very much.

Christ! It's setting things back. Can you see the guys from *Ti-Jos Marleau Antiques* wanting to take over the factory? They go to a PQ meeting, and there's Ti-Jos himself. No more fighting there? He's a good boss because he's a member of the PQ? We have to shake his hand? Christ! That's impossible! We'd be screwing ourselves.

If you don't stay in the party, you're not a real Québécois.

Whaddya mean, not a real Québécois?!

If you're not in the party or at least support it, you're not a real Québécois, according to them.

That's having the monopoly on nationalist feelings. It becomes a weapon against those who don't agree with the party.

Well, to hell with that party!

An Independentist Workers' Party

We have to create a party that admits there's a struggle between workers and bosses. An independentist workers' party.

A Québécois workers' party to lead the struggle for national liberation. They'll tell you you're dividing the Québécois, that you're doing the same thing the colonizers did to us — divide and rule.

I ain't making up the division. It's there. There's opposition between workers and bosses. Them that try to hide it are against the workers. I'm just interested in a party that recognizes the struggle and works on the side of the workers.

There aren't many of them. I'd even say there aren't

any in Quebec.

We got to make one. A workers' party.

. . . That can quite well struggle alongside the Parti Québécois for the independence of Quebec.

Sure. That'd shut up those PQ guys. We won't divide the Quebec people on the national question — both parties will be separatist. But we'll confront them over . . .

The ownership of the means of production.

We don't want no more English bosses, American bosses, but we don't want Québécois bosses either. We don't want bosses, period.

Okay, but what about your party—how do you form it?

Well look. The union centres that led the struggle in May, 1972 in Quebec could become a real party.

No. That would be a catastrophe.

Why?

A union and the centres formed by unions are organizations of workers to wage the struggle on the economic level, the struggle for better working conditions, wages, and all the rest. But these are not organizations to wage the struggle on the political level. Different jobs call for different tools. Last May, the centres carried on the struggle about as far as they could on the economic level. At the CSN convention the next June, they felt that the struggle had then reached the political level. So much so that Marcel Pépin suggested forming district committees to fight the Liberals in the next election. But they never got off the ground because the workers knew it just didn't make sense.

So you mean the unions should form a political party separate from their own structures?

I wouldn't advise that either. The unions could only come up with a social-democratic party.

What do you mean?

I mean a party like the NDP. A sort of English labour party. A Liberal party that looks a bit radical on the surface but in fact does not challenge the regime in any way. Ringing declarations on behalf of the workers, but a vote-seek-

ing party that will make any compromise to get into power
and govern in the name of the unions, U.S. unions at that!

Another doublecross in the name of the workers.

Yes.

**Yes, but don't tell me all union organizers are guys who're
going to sell out the workers . . .**

I didn't say that. The thing is that there's a difference
between union members and union organizers. The members are workers, who work. The organizers are those who
take care of organizing the unions and the Centres. A good
number are employed full time by the unions. And because
of the work they do, they tend to develop the habits of civil
servants in a big outfit, petit-bourgeois attitudes.

They don't have a capitalist boss any more. They no longer live the class conflict as workers do. They have a
"good boss," the union or the labour centre; their job is
"defending the interests of the workers." Their feet are
warm, they're comfortable. The trade union centre becomes just an institution among all the others in capitalist
society.

But the workers get fed up and decide to shake things up
a bit. We saw the Lapalme drivers occupy the CSN building in Montreal[1]. It's the initiative of the workers that
moves the unions, to action, on the economic level. It's the
initiative of the workers that ought to create the instrument
of struggle on the political level. Not the union. They can
help with moral, technical, and financial support, but it's
not for them to form or organize a workers' party.

**I'll go along with that. We always think we can't do it. We
always think it's just the bosses or else the union leaders who
got ideas and so can do things.**

---

1 The Lapalme mailtruck drivers are affiliated to the CNTU. They
occupied the CNTU Headquarters when it was about to give up
the fight against the Federal Government, which was going to replace the Lapalme drivers with non-union drivers. This action
forced the CNTU leadership to continue the fight.

Lapalme mail-truck drivers demonstrate on Parliament Hill, 1970 against the Federal Government's replacing them with non-union drivers.

The Role of Intellectuals

Only the workers are capable of forming and organizing a party that will not only defend the interests of the workers but also struggle to wrench power from the hands of the bourgeoisie.

We'll let in union organizers, people who are close to us guys . . .

. . . who haven't forgotten what it's like to be a worker.

Then the intellectuals, you'll see them tryin' to get in on the game, with their highbrow language. You gotta really watch those guys. Them and their theories. . .

Intellectuals . . .

O yeah, I forgot, *you're* an intellectual.

Oh, I don't know, when I see other intellectuals, I don't feel I'm part of their gang. I think it's because we identify intellectuals as mandarins or little high priests of the mind reigning over their domain and defending, by their attitudes and their whole ideology, the interests of a privileged class.

Those who come and tell us how to wage the struggle, without getting their hands dirty.

They can always take refuge in their universities or their studies.

They'd better!

But there is a group of intellectuals who have not done any productive work for a long time if at all, who sincerely want to join the workers' struggle.

Let 'em come. We'll test them.

These intellectuals should first of all learn from the workers. A guy can know all about social classes, their interests, and what's gotta be done but he has to be involved in day-to-day struggle. He has to test his theories in social practice.

I don't understand that.

You don't see it as a problem because you don't live it as a problem. Whatever you've learned, you've learned in day-to-day experience. There has never been any difference between what you do and the ideas you have. The class struggle between workers and bosses isn't something you discovered in a book. You discovered it in your daily life.

A guy who's been to college or university, has been taken aside and "given an education." Ideas to play with. Test-tube experiments to do. Experiments in the test-tube of bourgeois ideology.

Now let's suppose the guy wakes up, sees the whole structure he's caught in and the need for him to help change it. He gets to, this realization not through daily struggle against the bosses, but by discussions with other people. This discussion and confrontation of ideas leads him to see the class struggle although still in the abstract.

Let's say he now understands that the workers must organize to change the system. At this point, the mistake he'll make, most often, is to believe that *he* is the one to impart this truth to them, to politicize them.

Yeah. Snotty little punks telling us we're not fighting enough!

So, his first step towards understanding the concrete struggle of the workers is to join it. Not to tell the workers how to wage their struggle. Not to wage the struggle *for* the workers. But *with* them. To advance the struggle but not so far as to alienate the majority. To discuss the struggle with the workers. To apply the method of criticism and self-criticism.

You're still giving your intellectual a vanguard role.

To advance the struggle, we must organize effectively. To organize effectively, we need leadership that knows how to take the initiative and achieve results. If leadership is to be effective, it cannot be made up of what you call "intellectuals." They may have been intellectuals before. But once they are committed to the concrete struggle of the workers, they are simply politically conscious militants. As are those workers who have thought about their situation and knowingly committed themselves to the struggle. In fact, in a workers party, the intellectual-worker distinction would disappear and give way to a homogenous group of revolutionaries.

Okay, so you've got workers becoming intellectuals.

There's a language problem there. We don't mean intellectuals of the bourgeois type. We mean someone who is very aware, who sees things in political terms. Then you contrast these politically conscious persons to the masses of workers.

I think I understand . . .

You've seen bourgeois intellectuals in operation. Not in a party. That's understandable. At union conventions these leftists, 'intellectuals' as they're called, push through resolutions that the rank-and-file see as calls to civil war.

Yeah. Those guys got it all figured out in their caucus, then they bulldoze it past us in the full session.

You don't get that in a party.

You get it in the Parti Québécois, by Christ!

Yes, but the PQ is a membership-card party.

What do you mean?

You buy your card and you're a member. You don't even have to be an independentist. Three bucks and your John Henry, and there you are! So it's understandable that at the convention there are forty-six caucuses, left, right, centre, intellectuals, anti-intellectuals, pro-leader, anti-leader, anything you can think of.

Well, they discuss things.

So they discuss, and then what?

Resolutions come out of it.

And what does that change?

You got the party platform.

Hm, with something for everybody, something for every social class. Meanwhile, the leadership is playing the bourgeoisie's game, with the support of thousands of well-meaning independentists.

A Party of Revolutionaries

What kind of party do you want, then?

A party of activists who agree to begin with, not only on the independence of Quebec, but also on the struggle to be waged against the bourgeoisie.

A selective party, eh?

Yes. A political party that is not a social club. Not a debating society. But an instrument with which to change social structures. The complacency of a little club cannot be tolerated. It's not a refuge.

No bourgeois in a workers' party.

That's it. You're selective. Go on.

We only can take in workers, and other guys who want things to change.

Just any worker?

Well, no. Workers who want things to change.

There are lots of people who want things to change. But just wanting . . .

They got to be ready to take action.

Of course.

So the party is a party of activists and not a membership-card party.

That's right.

With a platform that defines the struggle to be fought against the bourgeoisie.

Objectives. Means to be used. That stands to reason.

Overcoming our Individualism

I think our big problem in Quebec is going to be that we're not exactly strong on organization.

That's true.

I mean, we have a hard time organizing a sugaring-off party.

That's because we've always been organized by other people. The colonial mentality.

You were saying that two hundred years ago under the French regime, we were independent of spirit, we'd bugger off into the forest if we didn't like the way things were. It's still like that.

Individualists to the bitter end.

We're not gonna get pushed around.

We do have a strong anarchist tendency. Doing our thing alone or with a small bunch of guys, making a little noise, getting noticed, that makes us happy. The effectiveness of the action isn't calculated, we don't even know afterwards if there's been a positive result.

That's right, dammit. It's the same in the union. Bang, bang, big declarations, people hammering their fists on the table, Jesus, it's a revolution! The next day we have a hard time getting three volunteers to distribute our newspaper.

That's all true, but lets look at it a little closer.

Anthropologists have found two characteristic forms of behaviour in our ancestors' cousins, the baboons and the chimpanzees. The baboons are a species of monkey having a well-developed social organization, with a super-baboon and all the lesser baboons below him. The ones on the bottom of the ladder are firmly in their place. When they meet an enemy, the males form a real army, under highly centralized command. They have a single soul. The individual no longer exists. It's the German army of 1940.

The chimpanzees are very democratic. No big chief, and when they're confronted with an enemy, they're no charging war machine. They scatter, but this is only temporary. Dispersal becomes counterattack, screeching, jumping around, taunting, quickly retreating, until the enemy gets tired and withdraws, or goes stark crazy. Guerilla warfare.

Well, we don't have the baboon tendency, that's for sure.

Indeed! We're rather chimpanzeeish. Quick outbursts, boasting, melting into the background, inflamatory speeches and then withdrawing to a summer cottage to recover. Then a surprise attack that surprises everyone, including ourselves.

Thinking about it seriously, which is more effective in the long run? Your baboons are big and tough. They may manage to win a battle, but with their rigid structure they're a perfect target. Your chimpanzees' will harass your baboons until they drive them crazy. They make their weakness their strength.

We're tough fighters. If only we could be more consistent . . .

There's even more to it than that. Think of it this way. The Americans, they are the baboons, the Vietnamese, the chimpanzees. It's how a small people defeats a bigger enemy. How a colonial people can defeat the imperialist monster . . .

There's also the fact that our goal is to do away with domination. You can't use the structures of oppression to do away with oppression.

We Québécois could make our weakness our strength!

More like emphasizing our strong points while overcoming our weaknesses.

We should have a strong organization, but a democratic one. First of all, with a voluntary membership.

I hope so.

We must study the principles of co-operation. Discussions, activities, criticism, self-criticism. Ongoing constructive criticism, to insure the participation of all the members and the development of leadership.

Yeah, that's all very nice. You can draw up the greatest plans in the world but if you don't have honest, dedicated guys in there, . . . If you have dirty doublecrossers, they can always pretend, look real good, and then bugger off when it's too late to do anything about it.

Yeah.

The problem is not making up nice democratic structures, or even putting them on paper. I think we could all do that. The problem is to find standards to judge people by, to see if they're there to serve the people or serve themselves. That's what I think is the big problem. You get a guy who says he's ready to work, who even works real hard, then all of a sudden he starts acting like a little dictator.

You can never know ahead of time. Finding out what people are like and helping them change — that's part of the struggle. Eliminating as you go along the hopeless opportunists, the parasites, and the paranoids. There's no guarantee. A guy can be good, he can think right, work hard, and then you find out his girlfriend's been telling everybody everything.

That's disgusting.

Yes, but it's part of the struggle. You have to keep in mind that your best workers at any time may change horses, and even turn up in the opponent's camp. And there's no sure fire way you can predict it.

I still think there must be a way to tell if a guy's going to cop out on you.

No. If you can find out what motivates him, maybe. And even then, people change over a period of time and not always for the better. You have to start with people who want to change. But as the struggle develops, the process of elimination enters the picture. Most people grow with the struggle, but some will not. We mustn't regard this association of individuals like a traditional marriage where people are tied together until death do us part. We must foresee in the very act of forming our party the possibility of divorce, and provide mechanisms to allow us to give the gate to guys who are hurting the movement.

PART V

Petit-Bourgeois Diversions

What's Bad and Good About Co-operatives

To overthrow the bourgeois order and establish a new order, socialism, the workers' party has to seize the state apparatus.

Better not count on elections to achieve that. The old-line parties run the whole setup. The government would indefinitely suspend elections if it saw that a workers' party might get elected. If you play by its rules, you never get out of the bourgeois-democracy-game.

Walkouts, strikes, occupations of factories, institutions, news media, cities, that's more effective anyway. *That* shakes up the government!

We can't just shake them up. We have to bring the government down, so that the workers' party can assume power.

First, people should understand the government ain't them.

I think they know it already.

So people should understand there's an alternative. They should start to exercise power.

The party has its work cut out for it there.

That's right. The party should show the alternative. Not just explain what power to the workers could mean, but take concrete action, set examples.

Not just examples. It should participate in creating this alternative.

We're not going to start setting up our own factories, are we?

Well, no. It couldn't be done. All the money and all the energy would go into a little factory that would be boycotted anyway when it posed the slightest threat to the local capitalists. And then, a bunch of workers becoming owners of a factory within the capitalist structures would soon start thinking and acting like bourgeois.

It wouldn't be the system that changes, but the workers. They would become petit-bourgeois. Just like the co-operatives. A bunch of people put their money together to set up stores or credit unions. It's small capitalism, and because it's small it looks harmless, even a good thing. But it's the capitalism of the little man, and it fits perfectly into the capitalism of the big bourgeois.

You mean that Cooprix or the credit unions ain't worth . . .

There are two sides to it. Take the members of the *Cooprix Co-operative.* They buy for less in their store, and have the feeling they're strong competition for Steinberg's. Instead of a single boss, or a management office in a large corporation, you have x number of members who are bosses with employees working in the store.

Well, that's something. The members make decisions. They participate.

Making a boss's decisions, participating like a boss, isn't that, rather, fitting into capitalism? Even if you and your bunch of people are wage earners yourselves?

Yes, but what if everybody's a member? Let's say everybody in Montreal is a member of one of hundreds of Cooprix co-operatives.

First of all, it's impossible. If Cooprix ever started to threaten Steinberg's and Dominion, the heavy artillery of big capital would be brought out, and there would be war. Cooprix would be wiped out. Big capital is never beaten by small capital. Co-operatives have never beaten the corporations, and they never will. But let's say for one moment that Montrealers are all co-op members. They buy everything cheaper in their Cooprix stores. What's changed?

We have a say in the prices.

They're going to use the same reasoning as the store-owners. They'll have to buy as cheap as possible, sell with a certain profit margin in order to pay the employees, to meet other expenses, and to be able to expand. You have just fitted thousands of people into merchant capitalism. They exploit the producers of commodities, and are themselves either exploiters or exploited in other areas of the economy.

So it's all worthless, then.

It's worthwhile insofar as the members see the co-operative not as an end in itself, but as a means of struggle against capitalism.

You just said they'd get wiped out by big capital.

Yes, if there's a confrontation. But if the co-op members are aware of the co-op's limits, they'll use it to accentuate the contradictions of capitalism. The co-op should help some people make ends meet. It'll serve as a meeting place and demonstrate the exploitation in ordinary business. It'll show how it is impossible for self-respecting people to go on in the present system, and point to the alternative. Just as the unions can only go so far without emerging into political activity.

When I say the party should take part in the formation of an alternative, I don't mean by creating parallel institutions, like factories, stores, or hospitals. No. It's first of all by organizing an information network, by publishing and distributing newspapers, books, magazines, and by setting up training courses. Giving leadership in the people's struggles. Helping to organize unorganized workers. You know that in Quebec only 35% of workers are unionized?

I know.

Helping students oppose their ideologically backward teachers, helping them set up parallel departments.

You mean like the School of Social Work at Sherbrooke?

Yes. A bunch of 300 students in Social Work took the lead in struggling against their profs and the reactionary administration.

It all started over marks, didn't it?

The students wanted to go on participating in the evalua-

Montreal Gazette
Demonstrators smash through a line of barricades backed up by
Montreal riot squad police during La Presse strike, Oct., 1971.

tion process, as they had been doing since the university was founded. The profs didn't want them to. The students boycotted their courses and went on with their education by inviting progressive professors from outside. They had never before learned so much. And in the course of the struggle, they were able to criticize the bourgeois teaching they had had up until then, and to understand how the present university serves to perpetuate the bourgeois regime, and how their chosen profession, social work, was just sticking bandaids on the contradictions in the system.

Some concluded that they shouldn't even become social workers. That must have been an eye-opener!

Many realized that their real role as politically aware people was to pursue the struggle against the bourgeois university, and once they were thrown out, as in fact happened, carry on the struggle against bourgeois oppression among the people.

A workers' party would have supported them.

Moral support, ideological help, technical aid, a network of information all across Quebec.

The party would be around to give a helping hand to local initiatives against the bourgeoisie.

Not only a helping hand. Criticism of their action. Placing their action in the context of the general struggle. Because the tendency is always to magnify your own action, and look at others through the big end of the telescope. The party should help local initiative, as you call it, to make the fewest mistakes possible, and take effective political action.

Right Opportunism: Social Democracy

The party must not fall into the trap of opportunism; and on the other it must avoid that other petit-bourgeois trap, ultra-leftism.

Starting with big words, eh?

You need words to identify different ways of acting. You see, the left . . .

What *is* the left?

The left is all those who want change in favour of the exploited.

That's a whole bundle of people . . .

Overall it is opposed to the right, which doesn't want anything to change because it's fine the way it is, or if it isn't, it should change in favour of the exploiters.

And then there's the centre, swinging between the two. Where do those names come from?

In the French parliament the members' seats were in a semi-circle around the prime minister. It just so happened that the reactionary parties were on his right, the progressive parties on his left. That's where the terms "right" and "left" come from. At least I think that's right.

So the 'left' takes in a whole bunch of people.

And a whole lot of parties. In France there are I don't know how many parties that call themselves leftist, radicals, leftist Gaullists, communists. Anyway, that's not a problem in Quebec yet. Let's hope it never is.

Instead of talking about parties, let's talk about major tendencies found in the left. Near the centre, you have what we can call 'bourgeois socialists' or 'social democrats'. They want things to change in favour of the exploited, but according to the rules of bourgeois democracy and bourgeois legality. They will vote-seek to the end. That is, they see the electoral struggle as the one and only means of struggle and their coming to power through bourgeois elections, never by other means. They are always tagging along behind the bourgeois parties in power which they criticize by proposing reforms. Reforms which are not bad in themselves, but which can always be made by the bourgeois parties, such as family allowances, health insurance, or old age pensions.

That's the NDP.

Which even refuses to call itself 'socialist', because that would 'scare off voters'. It's not surprising that they're opposed to other leftist movements whose claims go further than theirs. When they have come to power, as they have in Manitoba, Saskatchewan, and B.C., they behave exactly like a bourgeois party, but in the name of the workers. What difference is there between Schreyer's NDP government in Manitoba and Lougheed's Conservative government in Alberta?

In Quebec, we don't have a social-democratic party. The NDP is nothing . . .

There was the PSQ, the Quebec Socialist Party, during the sixties, but they didn't make too much noise. There were union organizers and intellectuals in it, but very few workers. It flopped first of all because there wasn't enough ideological work done to justify a party, and second, its platform was social-democratic (that is essentially reformist) not revolutionary.

The PQ *pretends* to be social-democratic. It wants unionization of all workers. It wants bigger allowances for widows, day-care for children of working mothers. It wants to nationalize the banks.

Social democracy is the most bastardized politics there ever were. Politics of the right, with appearances of being left. Opportunism. There are those who come to it from the true left. They're guys who really want change, but who are wavering. After a short time, they would rather have the piecemeal reform of a bourgeois government than continue the struggle and stick their necks out. That's what has happened in a lot of western countries.

But in Quebec, precisely because of the national question, social democrats mostly come not from the left but from the right. The nationalist bourgeoisie will adopt the style of the left, not from conviction but from *opportunism.* It's profitable in terms of votes.

They want to seize the State, not to change social structures and remove the State as soon as possible, but to preserve the State for themselves. State credit, State law, State police, will allow them to establish themselves as the bourgeoisie of Quebec.

And since they envisage the electoral process as the only means of rising to power, they have to seek a majority at election time. Their platform thus becomes an advertizing campaign to get votes. They have to present the State as a tool of the entire Quebec community. So, there will be fine resolutions on social progress, allowances here, grants there. A concoction to keep everybody happy.

No stands taken for the workers, but stands taken for social order. Handshakes for the dignitaries, but no support for those who might shake things up: that would be too dangerous. Promises in large numbers for people in general, but guarantees just for the people who count.

The PQ denounced the general strike in May '72 and the La Presse Strike the year before. And at the same time its leaders went off to New York to reassure U.S. capitalists on the intentions of a PQ government in Quebec City. That's the reality of bourgeois opportunism.

Okay. But before you go on, both the PQ and your workers party want to seize the State apparatus?

Yes.

The PQ, in the name of all Québécois; your workers' party, in the name of all Québécois *workers*?

Not "in the name of". The PQ may be able to take power "in the name of the Québécois", but it's certain that a workers' party will not take it "in the name of the workers." It's the workers *themselves* who are going to take the leadership in liberating all the Quebec people.

Wow! That's a heavy one. The good can't go wrong and the bad . . .

It's not that. First of all, the worker's party won't care about getting votes. They may sometimes participate in elections, but it would only be a temporary tactic. No promises, no bullshit to get votes. The straight goods. They won't say, "Come on in, it's fun, it's nice and warm, goodies for everybody." They'll say, "Struggle." "Class struggle." "Overthrow the bourgeoisie." It's not a picnic. It's not a sugaring-off party.

Yeah. That's a bit different already.

And then, it's struggles the party will be waging, not advertising campaigns. It will prove itself in practice. If it serves the working class, the workers will recognize it as their party. It will be the vanguard of the struggle. If it cuts itself off from the workers by becoming elitist, resting on its laurels, or adopting an opportunist line, there will have to be a housecleaning.

What if the vanguard browbeats the workers?

If it does, the workers will drop it. The 'vanguard' will then find itself just a stagnant little group. It'll no longer be the vanguard, just a navel-gazing political faction.

Workers' Liberation is the Key to the Liberation of All Mankind

You sure got a lot of confidence in the workers!

Yes, I'm not saying an *individual* worker. If you just take one guy at random, he could be completely screwed up. I've got confidence in workers as a class. They want to be free of exploitation. People don't like to be exploited. History is full of oppressed classes revolting against their oppressors.

Hey! What do all these people want with a workers' party anyway? Students, reformed intellectuals . . .

Transformed intellectuals.

What's in it for you guys?

The working class will lead the way to the liberation of *all* the classes oppressed by the bourgeoisie. You remember we said that the primary contradiction in capitalism is between the workers and the bourgeoisie?

You didn't put it quite that way . . .

Well anyway, the bourgeoisie, which owns the means of production, is capable of holding state power — and it does. And because they control the means of production, the working class is the only class with the ability to take over. Its emancipation is the precondition for the liberation of all mankind because it is only through its exercising its dictatorship that we can get rid of the oppressors for once and for all. For the first time in human history there will be a dictatorship of majority over a minority — real democracy.

That's bullshit. Domination has always existed and always will. The dominated becomes the dominator.

No. We said before that until human beings discovered agriculture there was no exploitation. Man was dominated only by nature. As he began to equip himself with tools to escape from this domination he undertook another. With agriculture, he truly began to turn the forces of nature to his advantage. But at the same time, he began to exploit his fellow-man.

Classes were born with the *division of labour*. Slavery saw the light of day. After that there was serfdom. Then wage-earning. But there is progress in all this. Simultaneous with class exploitation, and thanks to it, man succeeded in extending his control over nature. Today, he no longer needs to exploit his fellow-man to have a decent standard of living. Technology is now capable of eliminating most manual labour. Machines can not only maintain themselves, but in large part, manufacture themselves. Human ingenuity and the sweat of the exploited have brought this about.

But what calls for revolution is that in the capitalist world our social structures are of a former age. Capitalism, and now imperialism, with its private ownership of the means of production is completely outmoded as a social system. In many cases it cannot even make use of its own technological feats. It is the emancipation of the working class which will move us all forward to the next historical stage . . .

What people want is ice cream, a decent life, eh? Eating properly, having a decent home, working a little, having fun, not fearing for the next day or old age, not being terrorized by bosses, owners, the government, normal needs. And we can have all that, a hundred times over, with all the means and techniques of production that we have.

But because a bunch of god-damn bourgeois stick to the idea that greed brings happiness, they keep people from making their ice cream and eating it.

Yeah!

Yeah. Instead we have unemployment, the rape of our natural resources, water pollution, air pollution, pollution everywhere, perpetual insecurity, hatred between groups of people, wars like Vietnam.

Personal Liberation, Drugs

There are a lot of people who understand this. Many of our

youth understand. They're not going to sweat to live in utter poverty. Their slogan is "Ice cream now!"

Oh they holler loud enough. But they do bugger all. Just sit on their asses in the park and take drugs.

They've rejected the capitalist ethic that keeps us as frustrated as possible, selling us its trinkets, from snowmobiles to false eyelashes to vaginal deodorants to white Cadillacs. Young people's long hair, their jeans, their undeodorized bodies, their unfurnished pads, their 'families' of three or ten, their sexual freedom, their getting around by hitchhiking, their anti-rationalism, their non-verbal communication, their rejection of bourgeois etiquette, their anti-authoritarianism, their non-violence, represents their total rejection.

Yeah it's all negative.

It's okay — as long as they don't stop there.

It goes further, all right, but not in doing something. In destroying themselves, taking drugs.

Within the "youth movement" as it's been called, there are contradictions. It stands to reason. There are those who try to go beyond rejecting everything to a constructive stage. They start communes, parallel forms of social organization, communal farms . . . they either flop or just vegetate. Some then return to the existing structures, to try and help change them. Others sink into the delirium of an artificial paradise. And that's too bad.

It's disgusting; they got no guts.

Let's look at it in perspective. Line all that stuff up on a shelf: drugs that have been accepted for centuries, alcohol and tobacco, and the ones our western society has just "discovered." The whole bundle. Narcotics, stimulants, tranquillizers. Tea and coffee, too. Where do you draw the line?

Well, some ain't so bad. Like coffee and tea. Or a nice cold beer with a cigarette . . .

Someone else will tell you that pot is not harmful at all, and that the world looks nicer to him when he smokes it.

Yeah, well if just anybody's opinion counts for something, then some are going to want to have *everybody* tripping on

drugs. You absolutely got to have criteria.

Which criteria?

Well, I say if it helps to liberate the workers, it's okay, if it doesn't it's bad.

Some people will tell you that the worker who trips on LSD on the weekend *is* liberated.

First of all, what does he find on Monday morning?

The boss. The same exploitation.

And second, it's not individual liberation we need, it's *collective liberation*. Don't tell me if we all take it, we'll collectively liberate ourselves. We could be taking it with the boss on the weekend. Christ, you mean we'd all love each other? No way!

There's a guy who said to me that thanks to drugs, he could see Hitler as a decent person. And that guy was Jewish! With friends whose families died at Dachau.

I suppose if you told that guy you were going to gun him down, he'd say all right.

Yes. He's a vegetable. An ear of corn doesn't say anything when you cut it down.

He ain't human.

Human beings have a well-developed power of reasoning; grasping relationships and establishing distinctions, connecting and differentiating, so as to be able to act more effectively. The relationship between copulation and childbirth is not obvious. At a given moment, primitive man imagined this relationship, then verified it by experience. This discovery turned human relationships completely upside down. Today it allows us to control reproduction. Seeing in the falling of an apple the attraction between certain masses of energy, and developing from that the science of ballistics, is to imagine relationships, test them, and then apply the results.

This power of reasoning which develops by experience has led to science; the knowledge of relationships which are called "laws" and which govern the universe.

The power of rational reasoning has served on the one hand to develop man's control over his environment, and on the other hand to repress or harness human energy (the labour power of the workers) for the benefit of the privileged classes. But at the same time, this rational reasoning power, has enabled man to discover the laws governing societies. This is 'Marxism'. It is scientific reasoning that discovers the laws of human exploitation and indicates how to proceed to the next historical stage.

Yeah, but what do drugs have to do with all that?

The power of rational reasoning in the hands of the industrial bourgeoisie has been used to condition man as a producer, as a consumer, and as a product, with a view to maximum profits.

This rational framework has led to a revolt, which has shown itself not only in the workers' movement but also in poets like Rimbaud, who said that we must change our lives. You have to read *Refus global* by our painter Borduas[1] to see how one of our artists attacks the servile rationality he calls 'INTENTION' or 'CALCULATION'. He calls for a return to spontaneity . . .

And drugs are part of that 'spontaneity'? There you go again into outer space! What we need is to replace *their* rational reasoning with *our* rational reasoning, workers' rational reasoning. 'Marxism' you called it.

What's important, I think, is what changes the real world. And if drugs do change the world, is the change for the better or worse?

No. Capitalism's still here. Exploitation is still the same. On the contrary, drugs tend to blur the contradictions. They demobilize people.

So they're bad for the struggle.

Absolutely. And the reactionaries in power know it. In the black ghettos of American cities, when demonstrations are being organized,the hard drug pushers suddenly have almost unlimited supplies. You'd almost think the FBI was supplying them. But then the CIA's the biggest dealer in

---

1 Paul-Emile Borduas, a leading Quebec painter of the 40s and 50s who published in 1948 the *Refus Global,* a scathing attack of the repressive forces of Quebécois society and especially the church.

South East Asia. People can't fight when they are stoned. Drugs defuse the revolution. Leaders like Rap Brown have launched a large scale battle against drugs. Algerian liberation fighters shot drug pushers who didn't get out of the Arab quarters when they were fighting for their freedom from France.

It's the same with Quebec. The police are quite happy to see union and political activists tripping on mescaline, 'tho in public they condemn this 'scourge'. And just watch and see if during the next major confrontations there aren't all sorts of drugs available all of a sudden.

Drugs should be just for the sick, period.

Left Opportunism: Sectarianism

Okay, but remember quite a while ago we were talking about the opportunism of the PQ and the old PSQ . . .

That's right. Now, to the left of our party . . .

So in your left, there's a left and a right? Kee-rist!

Yes, To the left of your party, you can have a tendency that's called ultra-left.

That's the hard line.

No, not the hard line. It's the elitist sectarian line, which tries to count on a select hard-core group that acts *for* the masses instead of struggling together with them. It's a political line which wants everything done today, all at once. It's a line that violently attacks its friends and potential allies by denunciations and physical assaults. It's a line that in fact isolates the vanguard workers from the mass of workers. This gang considers itself, and defines itself, as the vanguard. But, the vanguard cannot define itself. It is the masses who define the vanguard.

The ones who start the party consider themselves the vanguard, don't they?

The founders of the party do not start by considering themselves the vanguard. They make an analysis of the situation, present a platform for action, and the means of taking action. It is the reaction of the workers in general to their proposals, the relationship that develops between

them and the workers that will define their role as vanguard, that will establish their leadership. The vanguard
can't be improvised.

Oh, there are some groups that start that way, but they
don't get very far. The MLP (Popular Liberation Movement) of 1965-66, and the FLP (Popular Liberation Front)
of 1968-69 showed this tendency. The FLP called itself the
vanguard. But it was only the vanguard of its own rear-
guard.

You still have little splinter groups today which show
signs of ultra-leftism. They baptize themselves and go off
to round up supporters. These are little political sects, with
their high priests, their rituals, their catechism, their dogma
and their 'persecutors'. But the Québécois are not rushing
to leave the old Catholic church to join these new religions.

You can't say the FLQ was a sect.

The FLQ had certain ultra-leftist aspects. Especially the
notion of the *select group* acting for the workers, in the
name of the workers, and not within the actual struggles of
the workers.

Those guys had guts.

That's the positive aspect. Some young Québécois had
the courage to commit acts that would compromise them all
to hell. They changed our traditional self-image — the will-
ing servant. But nothing changed in the way of power relationships.

It frightened the capitalists.

No. That is all wrong. The capitalists weren't all that
frightened. The Americans will tell you they have problems
like that all over the world, and at home too. "It's all part
of doing business", as they say.

Although it was just a part of the economic slowdown in
the U.S. that came with its defeat in the war against Vietnam, the recession in the Quebec colony could be blamed
on those "nasty FLQ scaring away foreign investment."
The actions of the FLQ served the Bourassa government's
propaganda purposes well. Got it re-elected. That's one negative aspect of the FLQ.

If the guys had had a base among the workers, it would've

The army on guard against the people of Quebec after Trudeau enacted the War Measures Act, October 1970.

made sense. I'd agree with that.

Not only a base. A party. It's most likely that the party would not have approved such actions.

So there would've been others . . .

Actions arising from the actual struggle of the workers.

An undercover gang with no ties to a workers' organization can soon be ten or fifteen different gangs, all using the FLQ name, all taking umteen contradictory actions.

Popular sympathy isn't enough. Anyway, the whole "elite group" outlook is wrong.

Yes, but maybe those guys would get fed up when they see nothing's coming of it.

Impatience has never been a strategy. It's a state of mind, which must be channeled into actions which only objective analysis of power relationships can define.

Not much room for spontaneity there. You were saying about Bourduas wanting us to get back to spontaneity . . .?

You were right. To change a society you can't just be spontaneous. Even in the arts you have to calculate, analyse the forces present. You're dealing with an enemy (the bourgeoisie) that doesn't want you to be free, and will use any means to stop you.

PART VI

The Role of the Workers' Party in the National Liberation Struggle

More on Overcoming Our Individualism

We're a long way from the structures we were talking about before.

Yeah, But all this is connected.

We were saying then that . . .

The structures of bourgeois society are structures of oppression.

A minority — landowning, factory-owning, bank-owning — the bourgeois impose their law on the majority who are working people. This is the dictatorship that has to be changed. But you don't change anything by patchwork reforms in the areas of consumption, housing, health care, transportation, or by forming parallel services like co-ops or clinics. Our party will support struggles on these issues because the immediate needs of the people must be met. And it is a good opportunity for us to meet other people and talk about not just a particular problem but the whole system.

All right. It's when the workers lay their hands on the means of production and you really start attacking the system. Then, well, the State intervenes and protects the property of the bourgeoisie. So, the workers have to acquire the tool to take over the State. That tool is the workers' party.

Yes . . . that's all very nice.

But in actual fact, I can't see a workers' party, We Québécois, the way we are, everyone for himself, independent, a chestbeater, we're not about to toe the line. You think you could find four of us who'd say goodbye to our summer cottages or our hunting trips or our snowmobiles to change your structures in Quebec?

Today, maybe not.

You think it'll be different tomorrow, and we won't be like your Canayen in 1885 who was cursing up and down at Sir John A. for hanging Riel, but all he did about it was vote for Honoré Mercier?

Conditions will make us different.

Conditions were pretty bad in the 30's, and what happened? The Canayen went to ask for help at the vicarage or at the government offices.

You have to have both. On the one hand the subjective conditions, awareness of class and the need for change, an understanding of theory; and on the other the objective conditions, an actual state of crisis, the sharpening of the contradictions of capitalism. Then watch out, bosses.

I tell you, we'd have to be as disgusted as we could be and then some. We'd have to be eating shit four times a day. And you'd *still* have guys telling you you shouldn't do nothing to rock the boat.

It goes back a long way. Since 1837 we've been grovelling, licking the boots of bosses and priests. You can't expect us to leap to our feet and run the mile in four minutes. We've just now managed to get to our hands and knees. That's really fantastic. Soon we'll be up on our knees.

Christ, you're discouraging! Here I thought we were at least standing up, a little shaky maybe, but on our feet.

I'm not making it up. You're the one who said Québécois don't want to face facts. I'm just telling you that those who don't are really still crawling on their bellies. But, there are a small bunch who are on their feet — including you. But you have to get everybody into the picture. That's the thing. Not just to see yourself, or see people through yourself, but to see people outside of yourself.

And to see yourself as another person among people. Not to grant yourself a privileged position.

Political awareness means seeing behind sometimes misleading appearances to the forces governing relationships between man and man and between man and the world. And to see them outside the feelings of dispair and injustice, outside of one's desire for justice, for love, or goodness. Seeing behind a personality or demonstration or behaviour the laws regulating them. You can never understand everything, but you can get a good idea if you don't let your feelings blind you.

Feelings. What've you got without feelings? Without feelings you're just a bundle of big ideas, an intellectual! There's just your lips moving! The rest is wood, dead wood, for Christsakes.

Who are you talking about?

Intellectuals who try to tell us what we are. As if we didn't know. Cold as ice. They stick us on charts . . .

What bothers you, the charts or the coldness?

Maybe just the coldness . . .

You have to understand that teenagers who've just discovered the world, and have the seeds of political awareness in them, take off in an intellectual balloon. But a guy who analyzes society is not lacking in feelings. He could have feelings of revolt, or of injustice. He could be damned opposed to bosses. But his feelings should not blind his understanding. If they did, he wouldn't be effective.

In fact, we're talking about the organization of the party in another way. What it comes down to is this: are we ready to overcome our individual feelings and get together with other people to make our actions effective, without killing each other's initiative?

Let me tell you, it'll be hard.

I know.

It'll work for two weeks, maybe a month. You mobilize guys for a strike. The guys are all with you. Then two or three weeks later, they cop out.

Look at the Common Front in the spring of '72. 210,000

La Presse

Montreal-area construction workers rally at Longueil arena during May 1972 General Strike, to vote on whether or not to return to work.

people stopped work .

Yeah, but where are we at today? The CNTU has been buggered.

Lost its virginity, you might say. Now the real work begins.

The CNTU has come a long way since it was the old Canadian and Catholic Confederation of Labour . . .

And its got a long way to go in building democratic, rank-and-file controlled unions in lots of cases. That depends on all of *us* doing our share. But at least we have a powerful national labour centre. That's more than English Canadians've got. The U.S. unions *really* run things there and that's a real problem.

The Quebec Federation of Labour's got American unions in it.

That's true and that's a problem. But more and more the Quebec locals of these unions are seeing that they've got to be independent of U.S. control if they are really going to fight for the workers of Quebec.

That's preaching hope, just like the priests do.

I'm not preaching. There are objective conditions. The CNTU[1] should renew its commitment and carry on the struggle, perhaps with reduced numbers, but politically more effective.

You want me to draw you a picture? We don't want to face facts. Who in Canada owes most to loan companies? We do. Who spends the most at Christmas for trinkets? We do. Who buys a cottage up north while still renting a house in the city? We do. Who buys the most snowmobiles? We do. Who's got the most freezers in their tenements? We do. Who lives way beyond their means? We do. If there was ever a people who jumped into consumer culture with both feet, with blindfolds on, it's us. We love gadgets and trinkets. We're kids, for Chrissakes! A nation of children.

Okay, we have no defenses against the capitalist hucksters.

---

1 In 1972, the right wing of the CNTU, frightened by the General Strike, called a meeting at which 75% of the 1200 there, voted to leave the CNTU, and create a parallel movement.

They could sell us packages of shit in Steinberg's, if it was wrapped in aluminum foil, for God's sake!

We're the best consumers in the world. We don't talk back. We buy everything that's for sale. Christ, we even steal from each other to be in style!

We're like the Indians, dammit, when the whites gave them bits of mirror in return for tons of furs. We're plugged into the U.S. Empire. They've stolen our forests and our minerals and now they're stealing our water and they've given us crap in return. We buy all the trinkets the Americans can manufacture, from minitractors to plastic vaginas.

That's what I said. We're Indians.

We're children.

It's our salvation.

Goddamned missionary!

A child, if he survives, is open. He can learn. And especially, he can create new things. Older people perhaps have some sort of order, but they're locked in.

So you think us Québécois, kids that we are, are going to make up new systems?

We're dazzled. Country bumpkins just down from our farms in the Laurentians. We flip, we trip out, we do handsprings. We're off and running.

That's right. Off and running. It's *over* by Jesus!

No, it's just beginning. We're out of the Sacred-Heart-of-Jesus orphanage. The next stage is to realize that buying trinkets is still being in an orphanage. The Free Enterprise Inc. Orphanage. We're going to realize that we're just getting screwed again, that the Chryslers, the yellow enamel kitchen sets, the all-terrain-aqua-snow-skimobiles, isolate and paralyse us just as much as the concrete walls with the crucifix hanging on them.

We'll drop it just as fast as we pick it up. Trinkets have to be paid for. It's the law of capitalist exchange.

But *we* are not going to pay. *We* don't want to spend our lives working like machines . . .

But if we're going to make it in the not-too-distant future, we're going to need organization, like we just said, and we're going to need unity. Unity among all the various groups that go to make up our Québécois nation.

National Minorities in Quebec

For instance, there's the workers in the various national minorities or ethnic groups. English-Canadians, immigrants — Italians, Portuguese, Greeks . . .

Yeah. Those guys are all screwed up. They come here to take away our jobs. If they didn't agree to work for less than us, okay. But they'll take 75c an hour! Us guys, we've got more self-respect than to work for peanuts in some sweat shop. We're unemployed while the Italians are picking up their crummy pay cheque and buying their duplexes and renting us their third floor! Shit!

It isn't the fact that they're Italians or Greeks that forces them to do that. It's the capitalist system and the government that protects that system. When things are going great guns, they need all the cheap labour they can get as well as the usual number of the native-born unemployed. If they don't have these two things, the workers could demand better wages and that would cut into profits. Business would suffer, And so the federal government, that great defender of capitalist interests, lures the unemployed from other countries here to compete with Québécois and Canadian workers.

The Italians and Greeks who have been promised the earth in the propaganda films — muscle cars, big houses, every imaginable gadget — arrive here looking for a job. They'll take whatever they can get. Because they *have* to. Most don't know that they're pawns in a capitalist chess game and that they're hurting the interests of all Québécois workers.

Oh yeah?

But once they get here, they're stuck here. You've got to remember they're *workers*. Objectively speaking, their interests are the same as the interests of Quebec workers. We must try to make them understand this.

They don't want to understand, the bastards. They come

here and make money by takin' our jobs and they don't give a shit for us. They want to make money, learn English, then go to California in their big Chryslers. Quebec for them is just a jumping off place.

All right, some do come here with their heads full of bourgeois dreams. We have to tell them that we're struggling against Quebec's colonial status and against the capitalist system. We have to convince them that they ought to join us, that they should become Italo-Québécois workers, *or get the hell out.*

You can't be Italian *and* Quebecois, come on.

Sure you can. The term Québécois refers not only to the Québécois as a particular national group, but to the Québécois nation. An ethnic group is a national minority group within a given country or nation. We defined nation at the very beginning of our discussion as people in a given territory, with a common language, and their own customs, and particular ways of seeing, acting on, and interpreting the world around them.

(By the way, the term 'French-Canadian' defines us as an ethnic group, a minority in a country, Canada, patched together a hundred years ago to better serve the British Empire. It explicitly denies that we are a nation.)

After the decolonization of Quebec the new nation, Quebec, will include all those living within its borders, the Québécois, the old French-Canadians, and all the national minority groups who would like to stay with us to pursue the struggle further. That includes English, Irish, Italians, Portuguese, Jews, West Indians, Africans, Chinese . . . those who choose to live in Quebec and plan to become citizens of the Republic of Quebec will become Québécois. Inasmuch as they keep their ethnic characteristics, they will be Portuguese-Québécois, Jewish-Québécois, Italian-Québécois, etc.

In the struggle for the decolonization and liberation of Quebec workers, individuals belonging to these ethnic groups will have to make a choice. To become Québécois and commit oneself to the struggle or at least be a sympathizer? Or to identify with the colonialist, the bourgeois power, and take the consequences.

Everybody's heard about St.Leonard.[1] But the newspapers won't tell you there's already a group of people from Italy who've organized to fight this very issue. The Italo-Québécois Progressive Movement[2]. They understand that they are in Quebec. They understand Quebec's struggle for national liberation and worker's liberation. They're with us. They speak Québécois.

Yeah, but how many of them are there?

There are maybe just a few hundred actually organized right now, but they're growing.

If all the immigrants are ready to do that, all right. If they're bourgeois they got no business being here. But, if they're workers and they understand what we're doing, they're welcome.

And that applies to all ethnic groups in Quebec. Even the Anglos. They know now that the Quebec nation is a reality, that the State of Quebec is coming, that the language in Quebec will be Québécois. It's up to them to decide, whether to become Québécois or to go and find their own kind in Toronto or Vancouver. Some English-speaking workers are also starting to understand that their fate is linked to that of Québécois workers and are disassociating themselves from the English bourgeoisie.

English bourgeois are feeling more and more uneasy. They're buying houses in Toronto, moving their head offices. There's the feeling that the picnic in Quebec is over. That's fine.

So you foresee all the ethnic groups dividing along class lines and deciding for or against the movement of Quebec workers?

For sure, and this will develop as we move ahead. Even the Jews, who are as touchy as porcupines on the subject

1 In 1968, in the Montreal suburb of St. Leonard, the school board decided to phase out English instruction in the elementary schools. The Italian population objected to this measure. Because of a lack of progressive leadership, the conflict degenerated into riots pitting Québécois workers against Italian workers.

2 A regrouping of revolutionaries of Italian origin, working at radicalizing the struggle among 150,000 Italian workers in Montreal. Their first success last year was a tithe strike that forced the churches to relax their financial hold on the Italian population.

of ethnic groups, will be obliged to recognize the class character of the struggle. The Jewish bourgeois will not be able to raise the cry of anti-semitism, because clearly we will not be discouraging them as Jews, but only as bourgeois. And Jewish workers will be invited to join our struggle.

I don't know many Jewish workers.

That's true — you don't see many these days in Montreal. They are now mostly in the liberal professions, medicine, law . . .

They **ain't workers.**

We wouldn't need lawyers if we weren't saddled with private property. But doctors and teachers perform socially useful work. In a socialist society, doctors and teachers are not privileged, but do play an indispensable role. In Quebec at present, doctors still do not see themselves as working people, *but teachers* are coming to do so more and more.

Look at the development of the CEQ. The teachers see that explaining what's really going on in the world to the growing generation is socially useful. They see that until now they've been playing the game of the dominant class and realize that they should begin to serve the majority of the population, the working people.

Getting back to the Jews. There are a lot of them teaching in the English schools. Some are beginning to understand that their interests are linked to those of Québécois teachers, and that they should dissociate themselves from the Anglo-Saxophone bourgeoisie.

We must rally all Quebec working people, all the workers of different ethnic origins in Quebec, around Québécois workers in the national liberation struggle.

After all that, you forgot an important group.

The Indians?

Yes, Don't they fit in with the rest?

No. First of all they're not immigrants. They were here when we whites arrived. Second, they were not originally part of western civilization. They share our heritage of slavery, feudalism, and capitalism only inasmuch as we've foisted it on them. They have never really known what it is, and probably don't want to know either. (Especially since under the circumstances, the whites were boss, and they were cheap labour.)

Their labour as trappers, hunters, workmen, farmers and fishermen is the foundation on which this country was built. But now they've been cast aside, relegated to a marginal role in our economy. And even if you offered them today the best of capitalism, i.e. let them be boss, they wouldn't want it although they do want a better life of their own making. The desire for exploitation is not in them, not a part of their mental makeup.

Okay, but here we are, with our civilization and all our machinery for exploitation.

Do we want to change it?

Yes.

So, we begin there. The Indians are here, we're here. We don't want civilization to equal exploitation either. We want to progress to the next stage in the human development. That's exactly why we're struggling against the bourgeois. Then we ask the Indians what they want.

They want big cars, lots of beer, and powwows.

And rifles to shoot the white man. Matches to set fire to the white man's schools. They look at the bottom of their beer glasses and see their people free, hunting and fishing, holding powwows without the goddamn white man to hassle them.

Basically, that's all *I* want, too.

I know. Let's start leaving them the hell alone. Leave them the territories they have now. Self-governing territories inside Quebec.

What if they want *all* of Quebec?

You're thinking of the claims of Gros-Louis[1], the Huron-turned-bourgeois who says he speaks for all Indians in Quebec.

Yes.

---

1 One of the prominent spokesmen of the Quebec Indian Association who claimed 4/5 of Quebec and offered to sell it back for a few billion dollars.

He talks like a landowning bourgeois, ready to sell what he's claiming as his. No, he's not a serious spokesman. We must talk to progressive elements in the tribes. Those who understand the whole system of exploitation of white man by white man, and Indian by white man. They don't talk about taking back Quebec. They can accept our staying, as long as we stop exploiting them.

What about *les Anglais*?

They can stay, but not as exploiters. Like we said before, there's no question of deporting racial or national groups. It's not a matter of the white men all going back to Europe, to satisfy an Indian nationalism, or the English leaving Quebec to satisfy Quebec nationalism. The struggle is not between races or national groups. The struggle is between classes and right now the class struggle and the national struggle come together.

That ain't going to happen right away.

It will take time, all right. But our party must work in that direction.

The Language of Quebec

So, all those people are going to talk French?

Québécois.

Québécois? No such thing. You mean *joual*?

Joual is an expression that means that our language is bad French, distorted French, just as the word *joual* itself is a distortion of the word *cheval*. Using the word *joual* to define our language is to place it in an inferior position, to compare it unfavourably with French as it is spoken in France. That is the colonial mentality again. Our language is the French spoken by five million Québécois.

You mean, what I talk is a real language? Come on now! With my 'goddamns' and 'Jesus Christs' every two words, you mean to tell me that's a proper language?

Very proper.

That's not what they said at school . . .

Language is a means of communication. But it's more

than just that. In class society, it's a means of oppression. Just like the police or the army. Know your place, old man! A cutting tongue is much more effective than a whip, boy! Take a child from the working class in France, who at home does not speak "proper French," whose speech is full of slang and pungent expressions. On going to school, he must adopt good French, the language of the Academie , the language of the French Republic, of the French bourgeoisie!

This language is a system of symbols with meanings precisely defined in an official dictionary. The poor little pupil learns to make the past participle agree with the noun, with no justification whatsoever, and write verb endings which are not pronounced. But these absurd rules, teach him to obey blindly, to do what he's told, because he's been told, period. He learns to set aside logic in favour of the absurd — BECAUSE THAT'S THE WAY IT IS — THE MINISTRY OF EDUCATION WANTS IT THAT WAY — WHAT? YOU DARE MAKE A MOCKERY OF THE REPUBLIC?

Shit! If there ever was a language that tried to confuse people, French is *it*.

Look at England, it's the same. Your accent classes you immediately.

Yes, but what about Quebec?

The Québécois language has been formed from regional languages of 18th century France. Put in some Normandy, some Parisian, and some Poitevin, toss with oil and vinegar, and you've got Québécois!

You mean French.

It has never been "official French." It is "bad French", regional French. Not the French of the ruling class. And this Québécois speech has persisted through two centuries of colonialism. (Our language as the language of a colonized people couldn't develop any more than we could.) When we were forced after the Conquest and the 1837 Revolution to accept our colonized condition and our inferior status, our language became 'dirt' in our minds. Just as the colonized Black sees his colour as 'dirty.'

Our elite — our intermediary with the English colonizer,

with its own colonized mentality — taught us a language from France they scarcely spoke themselves. What else could it become but the castrated language of a grovelling elite, the constipated French the priest and nuns speak. The petit-bourgeois graduating from classical colleges, doctors, lawyers, and notaries-to-be, pro-nounc-ed their lang-uage co-rrec-t-ly, to properly establish the distance between themselves and the common people.

They let us know that we were dirt, uneducated, uncivilized. They've protected us from the influence of those nasty British and Americans, so we could be culturally colonized by France! Enough explanation?

Enough.

Forget 'being proud' and 'talking proper'. Speak *your* language, say what you have to say in your own words, with your way of putting sentences together. Language in a class society is part of 'etiquette'. "Etiquette' is a way of keeping you in your place. Thank you. Good morning sir. Pardon me m'am. Pardon me ladies. Please.

That's why the first act of liberation is often using "obscene" language. Eat Shit "Bugger off". Yankee go home! It's shocking, it's not nice, it's nasty, it's vulgar. But it's indispensable. Revolution can't be polite. It must necessarily, by definition, be vulgar.

Vulgar?

'Vulgar' means 'of the common people', 'popular'. A popular revolution is necessarily a burst of vulgarity. Careful you don't get splashed, you nice people!

It's like clothes. As long as they make us wear white shirts and ties when we go out, and blue collars at work, we are stuck, we obey.

That's right. The whole code of the ruling class — language, dress, etiquette — has to be shattered.

I just thought of something. Trudeau uses bad language, and the people in favour of respect for Authority and the Establishment, they don't like it at all. He ain't playing his part like he should.

He's like all the traditional French-Canadian elite. Still a bit of shit on his shoes. After all, *rois-nègres* have a hard time being white.

So, we speak bad and it's proper.

Quite proper. And we have to start writing the way we speak.

The Youth Movement

Remember, we were talking about those people who are on unemployment, not because they can't get work but because they refuse to get caught in the vicious circle of the law of capitalist exchange. And these people, who we can call drop-outs, hippies, sneer at workers who work under the present system.

It's a fact that as we go along, the more machines replace workers, the less work there will be, and therefore the more unemployed . . .

But also there'll be more guys who don't want to go along with the system. They'd rather panhandle.

So on one side there's a bunch of workers who work hard and despise the unemployed and the bums. On the other there's the bums spitting on the workers, who after all give them a few crumbs so they can survive.

The first group is decreasing, the second increasing. And that comes partly from imperialism with its economic crises, forced underdevelopment and its highly developed technology and partly from total rejection by the exploited of the whole damn thing.

This is the result of the development of capitalism, the contradiction that Marx described one hundred years ago between productive forces and the relationships of production. The contradiction between the development of work techniques and automation on the one hand, and on the other hand the control by the few of the entire production process, first in one country and by now of much of the world.

This contradiction is now exploding. Vietnam, Laos, Cambodia, the Middle East, Africa, South America . . . Quebec. And it stands to reason that it should explode in

Quebec, because of the national question here. Although we (along with Canada) are a relatively highly industralized nation, we are part of the colonial world. We live beside the most advanced most powerful imperialist country in the world, the United States. Our economy is highly integrated into the metropolis. They consider us to be part of their "domestic market" for Christ sakes.

That, along with the sheer size of their investments here, makes us their most important—and potentially dangerous—colony. We weren't considered to be one of the hemisphere's "trouble spots" in the U.S. Central Intelligence Agency's Project Camelot for nothing.

Right now, objective conditions favour us. Unemployment, is always on the rise, one of the highest in the industrialized world. The government is giving away our resources for nothing, subsidizing foreign companies to come and take them over. And they're not creating any more jobs at that. Premier Robert Bourassa is hanging himself with his own rope. Poor caretaker. Sweep for them, be a doormat for them, lick the dust off their shoes, nothing helps. Boo-boo's caught in a vise.

So the federal government, to keep us quiet and keep us in this great land of Canada, hands out money to the unemployed and especially to our young people in the form of Opportunities for Youth and LIP grants. It means that these people can eat while having fun doing their "projects" as long as they don't do anything to rock the boat. But even these federal handouts can't go on indefinitely. Patching up the system won't work much longer.

It is absolutely necessary for a common awareness among workers, the unemployed and even the hippies to develop, as soon as possible. Workers can't go very far all alone. The unemployed collecting their unemployment insurance and at the mercy of the unemployment insurance commission are helpless alone. Those young people who have rejected capitalist society cannot just go on living the life of parasites on the system they are rejecting.

And they don't get far with their attempts at pre-capitalist small industry. Crafts, like leathercraft in the Square St. Louis village area of Montreal, or printing with a Gutenberg-style press on Laval Street. The trip right now is "ev-

eryone doing his thing". "Man, your trip is the class struggle. Mine's water-buffalo sandals." This individual trip
phase is quite normal. We've just been through the two or-
phanages; our wounds haven't quite healed. But there's another phase coming.

You want workers to start talking to "hippies"?

It doesn't matter what I want. That's the first step. Each
group should first of all understand what it is and where it
stands in the structure of society. That means discussion,
thinking, study . . . Then communication between groups.
Because even if they regard each other as enemies at first,
after becoming aware, they will see they're on the same
side.

I just can't talk to a guy who don't want to work. I can't.

Because he thinks you're an idiot to work, you despise
each other. If you can both overcome your feelings in political awareness of objective reality, you'll see you'll be
working together to change things.

**Just before you said that it was nice we were children,
now you want us to be grownups and overcome our feelings.**

"Grownups" in our society do not "overcome" their
feelings. They inhibit them. To protect themselves better.
No. We must honestly face up to our prejudices and fears.

Put some white kids and black kids together, or some
Québécois kids and English kids; they'll fight, knock each
other around a bit, then they'll become buddies, because
objectively they have no reason not to. And the only way
to keep up the hatred between them is to separate them, in
separate schools, separate courses, separate neighbourhoods. Leave them together and they'll mix so well the parents won't be able to recognize their own kids.

But put some Québécois from the east end of Montreal
together with some bourgeois from Outremont, and you'll
have a cold war, or a hot war, that will never end. What
can you do? Objectively they're enemies.

If workers talk things over with the unemployed and the
dropouts, they'll discover common interests and realize the
need for a common struggle. They'll overcome their differences.

Women's Liberation

What about women's liberation? You were talking a while back as if the women are even worse off than us workers.

I think so too. And it's true.

I can't buy that.

Do you admit that a woman is a human being?

Well, yeah. But she ain't as able as us.

Able to do what?

She ain't as strong physically.

In the first place, when you bring up a little girl to keep her knees together, wear a clean dress, and look cute, you're not going to develop her muscles, that's for sure. Anyway there is scarcely any hard work that cannot be replaced by machinery. There need be no physical work that a woman could not do (if it's that hard men shouldn't be doing it either). And what's more, women have more endurance.

They're not as good in business.

They're just as capable, but they are trained less than men to exploit other people. Now if you want to talk about democratic organization, women are often more competent than men. And tough! Look at the unions, when a woman gets in, watch out boys!

Yeah, that might be true but, if I'm not the boss with my wife, I feel I'm not a man anymore.

First of all, you're not really her boss. She puts you in your place now and then. But without this image that you're the boss, you'd feel you'd lost your manliness. That's because our society has always associated virility with violence and domination over women. If she becomes your equal, you think you've lost your balls, you think you won't be able to get it up anymore. Helping with tasks that she used to do by herself destroys your image of yourself. It's hard but it's worth the effort.

Let's leave my self-image alone for now. The problem is that women don't think like we do. They cry over notning. You can't give them any real responsibilities.

If a society treats half its members like children, they are going to respond like children.

The colonial phenomenon is similar. In Quebec, under the British we were taught to see ourselves as eternal hewers of wood and drawers of water, an inferior race, born to be slaves and indeed we were. Our prone position in turn confirmed English racists in their opinion that we were grovellers, servants, village idiots.

It's been like that for women since the dawn of civilization. Man established his domination over her, relegating her to babymaking and housekeeping, while he went out to conquer the world. He treated her as a child, an idiot, and then was able to justify this oppression by pointing to her child-like backward condition.

Women should be able to do everything men do?

Not so they can become the oppressors in turn. So that they can join men in ending the oppression of all mankind.

Equal pay for equal work?

Yes.

That makes sense. After all.

How about equal right to the same jobs as men. No more men's jobs, women's jobs?

Okay.

The same opportunities for promotion.

All right.

Liberation from the thankless tasks of housekeeping. Thus, day-care centres, sharing of housework. Abolition of marriage as a contract between a couple and the State.

What about the kids?

With all the contraceptive methods available, any children born will be wanted. A wanted child will be taken care of, without making up responsibilities based on guilt feelings. Responsibilities will be shared with society as a whole . . .

This business is kind of frightening.

It's frightening only inasmuch as you stick to present institutions, like marriage, for security. For sure if marriage is a refuge for you, where your wife becomes your mommy, and you become her daddy . . .you're not going to want to throw it all over, even if you hate each other as man and woman.

I don't find it's like that.

You still love each other the way you did when you first met?

No, that's for sure. Sometimes I feel like another woman now and then. But she *is* my wife.

That's right. You stay with her because she's a piece of property, very reassuring to you, just like owning a house or a car. She gives you security.

Uh, can we change the subject?

No dammit. I'm not saying that it's you particularly. Traditional marriage has been a safety valve for our society. Bourgeois marriage reproduces the structure of economic domination, with the man, exploited at his place of work, becoming the exploiter at home. He can bang on the table and get his revenge for the daily humiliation of his crummy job. Marriage is an outlet for his thwarted energy. But it's more than that. This economic unit, the nuclear family as it is sometimes called, is absolutely necessary to the capitalist economy. It is the unpaid labour of the housewife that makes it possible for the husband to go to his job and it is the unpaid labour of the mother that raises the next generation of workers.

The love affair has been dead for a long time, if it ever existed.

You're in favour of free love?

Love is always 'free', by definition although by 'free', I don't mean without responsibility. If you lock love up, it will free itself or it will die, bit by bit, week by week.

The trouble with 'love' in a capitalist society is that it is always seen on an individualistic basis. Love for oneself. Love for one, particular individual. Not as love for the people.

Love is seen as an end in itself. The hero and the heroine ride off into the sunset. It is not a means to an end or a

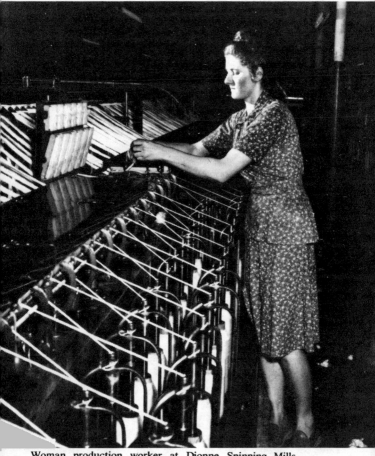

Woman production worker at Dionne Spinning Mills, St. George Beauce County, 1948.

part of a process, the process of building a new society . . .

That's why so many people we know are all messed up!

If a guy needs a mother, let him find a mother, or his own, but at least he shouldn't impose this role on the woman who he is supposed to be in love with. Women have enough trouble being mothers to their children without being mothers to their husbands too.

So you want men and women to get together and break up just like that.

To get together when they both feel like it, and to break up when things aren't working any more.

That's like a whorehouse.

It's simply mutual respect. And whorehouses will disappear with free relationships. Women stuck in their kitchens at home, women we call decent, are now realizing that the women in whorehouses are not their competitors but their sisters, and that both are stuck in structures of exploitation that have kept them from meeting, uniting, working for liberation. Women are not going to be pushed around any more. Watch out.

Christ! You can see revolutions everywhere! Of Québécois as the colonized, of workers as the exploited, of women as . . .

. . . cretinized, colonized, exploited, and oppressed. Yes! And the Québécois working woman is triply exploited. As a Québécois, as a worker, and as a woman.

Don't you think one struggle at a time is enough?

Which one has priority? Go ask the woman. For the petit-bourgeois Québéois, independence comes first, social problems second. For them nothing comes third, as women just need a little help to get ahead. For Quebec workers, social problems come first, independence second. For them, women just have to make their own way. But some women who have been involved in political organizations— as typists and dishwashers—now say that the woman's question must come first, independence and social problems second.

Everybody's off in different directions . . .

National Liberation

Yes. The tendency right now is for each group to put its
own interests first and refuse to unite with the others.
That's not surprising. But it is crucial now for each group
to realize that the next step is to work out a way they can
work together. Because in fact all of their interests will be
served by the liberation of Québec.

**It can't be done. I don't want any emasculating women
and I don't want no petit-bourgeois independentists
either . . .**

The Patriotes of 1837, they were trying to make a bourgeois democratic revolution and they failed because they
just didn't have the economic power. Well, history isn't going to give them a second chance. In the age of imperialism
there's no such thing as an independent capitalist country.

René Levesque and his little-big bourgeois? They aren't
strong enough and they won't ever be. They'd be in the
American's pockets in no time. Or the CIA'd be up here
dumping Levesque like they dumped Salvatore Allende in
Chile.

If we're going to liberate Québec, all of the Québec people, we're going to have to do what they've been doing in
the rest of the colonial world. Fight a war of national liberation.

I thought all we had to do was organize the workers.

Workers will be the leading force but they can't do it all
on their own. There are a lot of people who want to get the
Americans out, who want liberation and who aren't workers. Farmers, for instance.

Yeah, farmers, hospital workers, teachers, students . . .

We'll need everybody, even people we'd call "progressive" bourgeois. Remember we said that most of the bourgeois of Québec weren't really a bourgeoisie at all? They
own things, alright. But they don't really run things here.
The real bourgeois are the Americans.

So we'll be uniting with them? With "our bourgeois"?

Remember, once the bourgeoisie was *the* revolutionary
class. "Our bourgeois", the guys that feel just a bit that

they're Québécois, that aren't completely dependent on foreign capital, they still have certain revolutionary aspects. After all, they're getting screwed by the Yanks. At certain periods and to a certain degree they'll be with us and they'll help.

That sounds to me like the Parti-Québécois all over again. All Qué-bé-cois together . . .

Not at all. René Levesque says, "C'mon everybody, join. So you and me join and what do we find? The big shots, petit-bourgeois, bourgeois, intellectuals really running things. Oh, workers can knock on doors at election time and give money and vote for it. But to get the PQ to do anything for working people, well, we have to fight all the way: caucuses, backroom deals, threats, confrontations. We spend all our time playing games just to get the smallest things . . .

That's why we need our own party . . .

You remember I said we're going to have a national liberation struggle? Well, in Vietnam what they did is get everybody together. Everybody who wanted to get the Americans out, that is. But not in a party like the PQ. In an *organization of organizations* which they called the National Liberation Front of South Vietnam.

You mean like the "Front Commun"?

Yeah, that's it. Three union centres got together to fight a common enemy — the Québec government. But they didn't give up their existence as separate organizations. They said, we'll unite our forces on the basis of certain principles — one — two — three — and we'll work together to achieve a goal that's in all our interests. That's how far it went. Does the Front Commun exist today?

Nah, nobody agrees on anything.

But the Front Commun did strengthen the workers in fighting the government while it lasted . . .

In Vietnam, all sorts of groups belonged to the NLF, political parties, student groups, women's organizations, religious organizations, trade unions. Organizations of every kind as long as they were ready to fight the imperialists. They got together and drew up a programme they could all agree on. It didn't contain everything everybody wanted and some of the groups probably found some of it hard to swallow. But everybody agreed that the most important thing was to get everybody together into a fighting organization . . .

And it worked? All those different people?

They brought the mightiest army in the whole world to its knees. It just couldn't beat them. But the students alone couldn't have done it, or the workers or anybody. It took the whole united Vietnamese people . . . determined to overcome their differences . . . to win.

Do they have a workers' party in Vietnam?

Yes.

So our workers party'll just be part of the Front? Won't that mean going along with things we don't like? Divert us?

Insofar as the workers' party can work with other organizations and progressive individuals, the workers' struggle for socialism and the struggle of the whole people for liberation will be strengthened.

But workers must not, under any circumstances surrender control of the strongest weapon they have — their party. If they do, it's back to the PQ again.

If the national liberation struggle is to be successful, it'll have to be the leading force in the Front.

You mean our "good bourgeois" are going to let us lead, just like that?

Our workers' party isn't going to "lead just like that". Just like anybody else, it'll lead if it leads. If it doesn't, too bad. Too bad for the Québécois workers, too bad for the whole Québec people, too bad for the struggle in Canada and the rest of the world. But nobody's going to stand up and say "Step right up, we saved the top position just for you". The people will judge and they'll judge by what we do.

The reason the struggle needs the leadership of the working class and its party is that potentially it is the strongest class. And with the power of rational reasoning, the science of Marxism that we were talking about, it is the only class that really understands the struggle in its entir-

ety. It is the only class in whose interest it is to see the
national liberation struggle through to the end. It is the only
class with the discipline and organization to lead the whole
struggle to victory. It . . .

**Okay. Okay, Sounds great. But if you ask me, we just
can't trust those Ti-Jos Marleaus. If they have to choose between the Americans and capitalism on one hand and Québec
and socialism, workers running things, on the other hand . . .
they'll be the first to salute the flag and whistle *Dixie*.**

Some will, some won't. They'll be sorted out in the
course of the struggle just like everybody else. But that
again explains why we can't leave the leadership of the
struggle for independence in the hands of the Parti-
Québécois. Carrying the struggle through to the very end is
only in the interest of the working people, not the bourgeois.

So what happens when we've gotten free?

Rid of the foreign bourgeoisie that runs Québec — taking over their property to be administered by the Québec
people . . .

That's when we get socialism?

All the groups who fought for liberation will form a government and the task of building a new Québec will really
begin. In China and Vietnam they called it new democracy.

That's socialism?

No. We'll have to deal with the local bourgeois over the
next period of time. That's when the struggle for socialism
will become primary.

**You mean that first the struggle for independence is pri-
mary . . . ?**

Not independence. More. "National liberation". But,
yes. First national liberation. Then socialism.

So, what's our party doing now?

All along we've been developing the trained and dedicated people, organization, theory. Everything we'll need
to really change Québec society. It will have to be very
vigilant to preserve what has been won, to see that the imperialists don't get somebody to let them back in through
the back door. But its main task now is the achievement of

socialism . . .

What you *really* mean is "communism".

No, "socialism". That classless society we were talking about is still a long way off. Socialism is an intermediate stage, that new kind of dictatorship we were talking about. The dictatorship of the majority - the exploited - over the minority - the exploiters. Marx called it "proletarian democracy" or the "dictatorship of the proletariat" to distinguish it and contrast it with "bourgeois democracy" and the "dictatorship of the bourgeoisie". "Communism" is when there is no longer any need for dictatorship because there aren't any classes left, no more structures of oppression at all. There's complete democracy. But we've been over this before.

But what about the women, won't their struggle just get lost again?

Women will have to form a caucus within the party, lead a fierce struggle within the party itself against male chauvinism, and to take leading positions in the party. You say you support 'equal pay for equal work.' Women will only start to really have a say when they can get the same jobs men can get. When there are no more "women's jobs". When women play an equal role in the productive forces in our society. On the job.

That's it goddammit, hang onto their skirts! A minute ago you tell me not to take my wife for a mother, now you're tying me to her apron-strings. Hold on there!

First of all, she's in the process of taking off that apron, and putting on pants. It's going to be two people equally attached to each other, two human beings both wearing pants, who respect each other as equals in all fields.

Because women are exploited three times over, you're giving them a leadership role. They're going to be telling us what to do.

It's not a case of that. The leadership should assume these three struggles. And although women are the most knowledgeable on the subject, because they live the struggles every day, there's nothing to stop an aware and dynamic man from taking on women's struggle as well as the other two.

All right. But if there was a capable woman, you'd let her run the whole show, eh?

Certainly.

You think she'd be able to do it?

Oh, come on.

Well, Jesus Christ!

Wait until women come along. You'll see, you're going to accept them, faster than you think.

All right. I'll wait and see!

True Internationalism

Come on. Nobody wants to face facts. You can't do nothing.

Right now we're in a slack period but you can't say nothing's happening just because things are quiet. A liberation movement is a living organism. It develops gradually, systematically. But it also has its highs and lows. Its rhythms. For six months, there'll be feverish activity, everybody working at full speed. Then it'll drop off to nothing and seem dead for six months or so. Just like you. You work, you rest, then you get up again to go to work.

But during the calm there is thought going on. Assimilation of the political experience acquired during the active months. Building and strengthening organization.

We're not going to have a general strike every year. But there is always something happening. The strike at United Aircraft, Firestone. The growth of the Comité de Solidarité . . . It's not over.

I'd really like to believe you.

Look at what's happened in Quebec in the last ten years. McGill Français, the St. Jean Baptiste Day Riot, the FLQ, the War Measures Act, the Gars de Lapalme, the Murray Hill thing, the police strike, the La Presse strike, the teachers' strikes, the General Strike . . . Look how far we've come!

If you look at it that way . . .

It's the only way. We must always see our actions in the

widest possible perspective of space and time. That means in terms of the world-wide struggle against oppression and in terms of the historical development of all mankind—especially in the 20th century.

Our liberation movement in Quebec is part of the world-wide movement against the bourgeois, against imperialism. Colonial peoples are standing up and saying that they have had enough. And the imperialists are having to back down. But it isn't easy and it takes time. Look at how long the Vietnamese have been fighting and it isn't over yet. They haven't given up because in the long run, they know they'll win. It may take a few more years. It may take twenty years, but they're going to make it.

Look how long and with what slim resources the liberation fighters in the Portuguese colonies in Africa have been fighting. The Portuguese just couldn't take it any longer and now they're backing off. And that gives hope to their brothers in South Africa. Our brothers . . .

When you keep things in perspective, when you know where you are and where you're going—then you can make good use of the slack periods.

Yeah. But in the meantime, your party . . .

That's why we need our party. To give us the perspective we need and the continuity. Right now we should be preparing the ground so our party will have a solid basis.

So you really believe that a party is indispensable?

Without it we'll have nothing. The party is our most powerful instrument of political struggle. It is the indispensable support for long term and effective political work.

Yeah, but you just can't get around the fact that we don't like organizations much.

We'll still have to have one. Not just to coordinate the struggle within Quebec, but to maintain relations with foreign organizations sympathetic to our cause. In English Canada there is a liberation movement being organized.

Can't be.

Yes sir. There are Canadians who understand, who are

struggling for an independent socialist Canada just as we're struggling for an independent socialist Quebec.

You mean there are people who are awake in Toronto?

In Winnipeg and Vancouver, too. And these people agree that Quebec should separate if it wants to.

That's encouraging.

That's what I've been trying to tell you. If you keep informed, if you're aware of all the liberation struggles going on, you feel less alone. Then, you can communicate with them, talk over common difficulties, different means of struggle. Especially we have to remember that we Québécois, Canadians, Mexicans, Puerto Ricans — and American blacks, workers, Mexican Americans — have a common ENEMY, U.S. IMPERIALISM. Canada, like Quebec, is a colony of the American imperialists. It is in both our interests to work together.

But not in the same country.

At present, the political structure of the State or Country of Canada alienates and oppresses the Quebec people. It robs them of their rights as a nation. And the Canadians who are also caught up in this structure, which was set up by the British imperialists when they ruled Canada, are in the unhappy position of being used to oppress their brothers in Quebec. For the benefit of the American ruling class.

This political structure must be destroyed. And progressive elements in Canada quite realize this. But it can only be destroyed if we two peoples work very closely together. Even though Trudeau is just a front man for the Americans, the Canadian army is the first line of defense for U.S. interests in both Canada and Quebec. We'll both be stronger if we fight that army together . . .

But most English-Canadians look down on us.

Because they're taught to. Remember, we said that the English bourgeoisie used the priests to keep we Canayen in our place? Well they also used English-Canadian workers — but outside of Quebec. They taught those guys to call us 'frogs' and 'pea soupers'. You know the bit. Promoting hatred — we call it national chauvinism — to keep workers from the two nations divided. To have a majority in English Canada to vote in their phoney elections to keep the

Québécois in their place and keep them from "wrecking Canada".

You mean the bourgeoisie is just using these guys?

You see how vicious it is. And it's not easy to change. It's one of the hardest things our friends in English Canada have to fight. And if they aren't successful, it will be very serious.

The smartest thing the Yanks could do would be to get us fighting each other . . .

And that's just what they tried to do during the so-called October Crisis. Things were getting hot in Quebec and so Trudeau sent in the troops telling English Canadians that he had to do it to 'preserve national unity' so they wouldn't be taken over by the Americans. Using Canadian patriotism to put down the Québécois to keep the country quiet so the Yanks can run all over both of us . . .

Wow, you've got to give those guys credit . . .

Well, it's worked for two hundred years . . . But it's not going to work much longer.

Not if we know what's going on and the guys in Ontario know . . . Then they won't be able to use us any more . . .

One more thing about your friend Levesque.

My friend Levesque? Hey wait a minute . . .

The phoney independentists, they use Trudeau's trick too.

They do?

Yeah. What do you think it costs to stand up to a puppet like Trudeau? to the big boogie men in Ottawa? While everybody was calling those guys in Ottawa names including the Quebec Liberals, Bourassa was giving Rockefeller the north shore of the St. Lawrence. And Levesque was flying to New York. While they're taking cheap shots at Ottawa, whipping up the national feeling of the Quebec people, they're all making deals with the Americans.

Ottawa is just a side show. We've got to put an end to Confederation, that's right. But we've got to keep in mind who the real enemy is. And keep a real close watch on guys squawking about 'Ottawa'. The main thing right now is getting ourselves together to be ready when the crunch comes.

The important thing is to strengthen our organizations in each nation and to work together when the struggle demands it.

Talking French?

Speaking Québécois when they come to see us in Quebec, speaking English when we go to see them in Canada.

That's all right by me.

Relations like those between any two self-respecting nations. They'll invite us to come and explain the progress we've made. We'll go and tell them, in English, in Toronto, Halifax, Vancouver. We'll invite them to Quebec, they'll speak Québécois . . .

Well, they'll try . . . !

What you've just described is a long way from the old anti-English, anti-English Canadian, we'll look after ourselves-thank-you . . . attitude.

That's true. It's a progressive nationalism, opening outward to the world, recognizing the existence of the rights of other peoples as it demands the rights of its own people. It is a nationalism which understands that it is not people as individuals or as members of national or ethnic groups that are their enemies but rather, that it is social structures that are the problem. Mao Tse Tung summed it up really well, "In wars of national liberation, patriotism is applied internationalism".

Yes, but you can't change social structures without throwing the whole world into chaos.

True. The bourgeoisie in every country is going to get it. But it's necessary to keep in mind that it is the *class* that we will eventually destroy. All bosses. English-Canadian, American, Québécois. It's a world-wide struggle.

In each actual struggle, a strike at Steinberg's for instance, to denounce the boss because he's Jewish or you don't like the shape of his nose is to fall into the old trap of national chauvinism or seeing the enemy as this or that *individual*.

Calling someone a bourgeois. That's the worst insult!

St-Jean-Baptiste demonstration, June 24, 1971. The police insti-
gated a riot during the Québécois national holiday celebrations.

Canadian Liberation Publishers

NC PRESS is the publishing arm of the Canadian Liberation Movement. It is truly a people's publishing house, distributing books on the struggle for national independence and socialism in Canada and throughout the world.

The History of Quebec - A Patriote's Handbook
1. Léandre Bergeron   English $2.50

The History of Quebec - In Pictures! No. 1 & 2
2. Léandre Bergeron & Robert Lavaill   English $1.00

More Poems for People
3. Milton Acorn   paper $2.25
4.   cloth $5.00

Why is Canada in Vietnam?
5. Claire Culhane   paper $1.95

The Trade Union Movement of Canada, 1827-1959
6. Charles Lipton   paper $4.95
7.   cloth $9.95

1837: Revolution in the Canadas,
as told by William Lyon Mackenzie
8. Greg Keilty (editor)   paper $2.25
9.   cloth $5.95

The History of Painting in Canada,
Toward a People's Art
10. Barry Lord   paper $6.95
11.   cloth $11.95

Black Canadians - A Long Line of Fighters
12. Headley Tulloch   paper $3.95

Petit Manuel d'Histoire du Québec
13. Léandre Bergeron $1.00

Histoire du Québec Illustrée No. 1 & 2
14. Léandre Bergeron & Robert Lavaill $1.50

Pourquoi Une Révolution au Québec
15. Léandre Bergeron $1.00

L'Histoire du Québec en 3 Régimes (play)
16. Léandre Bergeron $2.50

Les Révoltes d'Acadie
17. Pierre Godin $1.50

It is particularly important for people in Canada to read books from Quebec. To understand the growing struggle there and learn from the rich culture and literature which is developing in the course of their liberation movement. NC Press distributes books from Éditions Québécoises, Éditions de l'Aurore Parti Pris and Ré-édition Québec.
Complete catalogue available on request.

NC Press is the largest Canadian distributor of books, periodicals, and records from the People's Republic of China. Available are books on all aspects of developments in China today, as well as the works of Mao Tse Tung, Lenin, Stalin, Marx and Engels.
Complete catalogue available on request.

NC Press has recently become the Canadian distributor for the national publishing house of Tanzania. Tanzania Publishing House is now well established as the major publisher of books in Swahili and English both for the student and the general reader.

Box 4010, Station A, Toronto, Ontario 368-1165
Please send me the books whose numbers I have listed below.
I am enclosing $..... (Please send cheque or money order).

Please send me a catalogue of NC Press publications ......
From Quebec..... From China...... From Tanzania.....

Name...

Street..

City ....Prov.....

NEW CANADA

NEW CANADA, is the Canadian liberation newspaper, that reports on the struggles being waged across the country for Independence and Socialism.

NEW CANADA has exposed the injustices of the U.S. stranglehold and explained how Canadians are fighting back - to win! - in stories like these:

- *The Great Anti-Lead War Continues*
- *Developing a New Canadian Culture*
- *Canada Must Have Canadian Universities*
- *Congratulations to the Founding Congress of the Canadian Workers' Union*
- *Big Gains for Canadian Unions in B.C.*
- *Women's Liberation is Essential for Canadian Liberation*

Regular features include *People's History,* the repossession of our past, and *People's Art,* a step toward a new Canadian culture.

New Canada, Box 6088, Station A, Toronto, Ontario

Sub rates: 10 issues, 1 year: $3.00
           20 issues, 2 years: $5.50
           50 issues, 5 years: $13.50

Enclosed   please   find   a   cheque   for
$..........

Here   is   a   donation   to   help   New   Canada
$..........

NAME ....

ADDRESS ....

CITY ....PROV..............

Join CLM !

Date Due

Canada is a colony. Our ———ue unions, our natural resources, our culture, our universities and our industry — all are controlled from the U.S. There are those who, seeing the extent of this colonialism, believe the battle to be lost. We do not see it that way. We see people across the country rising up against U.S. imperialism: workers struggling to forge militant, democratic Canadian Unions, farmers fighting U.S. agri-business, students opposing the takeover of the universities by increasing numbers of American professors.

JOIN THE CANADIAN LIBERATION MOVEMENT! Join the fight for independent rank-and-file controlled Canadian unions. Participate actively in the struggle to free Canada from U.S. imperialist control.

The CANADIAN LIBERATION MOVEMENT is devoted to building an independent, socialist Canada. It is up to you and to every progressive and patriotic Canadian to become involved to the extent of your resources and abilities in the saving of our nation and in the building of a new and better Canada.

To: CANADIAN LIBERATION MOVEMENT
    Box 41, Station E, Toronto, Ontario 964-1139

Please send me more information about the Canadian Liberation Movement . . . .

I want to join CLM . . . .

Here is a donation of $. . . . . . .to help you with your work.

NAME . . . .

ADDRESS . . . .

CITY . . . . .PROV . . . .